MONTY ROBERTS

THE HORSES IN MY LIFE

Trafalgar Square Publishing

*I dedicate this book to my grandchildren, Matthew and Adam Loucks;
and Loren Frances Roberts, daughter of my son, Marty, and Heather Roberts.
This is a part of your heritage. And I can't leave out our extended family,
the foster children who have also enriched our lives. I hope all of you enjoy
reading these special stories about the horses in my life.*

First published in the United States of America in 2005 by
Trafalgar Square Publishing
North Pomfret, Vermont 05053

Published simultaneously in Canada by Random House Canada, a division of Random House of Canada
Limited.

Originally published in the United Kingdom by Headline Book Publishing, London, in 2004.

Disclaimer of Liability
The author and publisher shall have neither liability nor responsibility to any person or entity with respect
to any loss or damage caused or alleged to be caused directly or indirectly by the information contained in
this book. While the book is as accurate as the author can make it, there may be errors, omissions, and
inaccuracies.

Library of Congress Cataloging-in-Publication Data

Roberts, Monty, 1935–
    The horses in my life / Monty Roberts.
        p. cm.
ISBN-13: 978-1-57076-323-6 (hardcover)
ISBN-10: 1-57076-323-2 (hardcover)
1. Horses. 2. Horses-Behavior. 3. Human-animal communication.
I. Title.

SF301R58 2005
636.1—dc22

Endpapers: David Stoecklein/Corbis
Title Page Photograph: *Monty and Johnny Tivio at a cutting competition, Tucson, 1966*

The author has made every effort to contact the photographer of the front cover image, however this
person's identity and whereabouts are unknown. Should the photographer's name become available,
he or she will be credited in future editions.

Printed and bound in the United States of America

10   9   8   7   6   5   4   3   2   1

CONTENTS

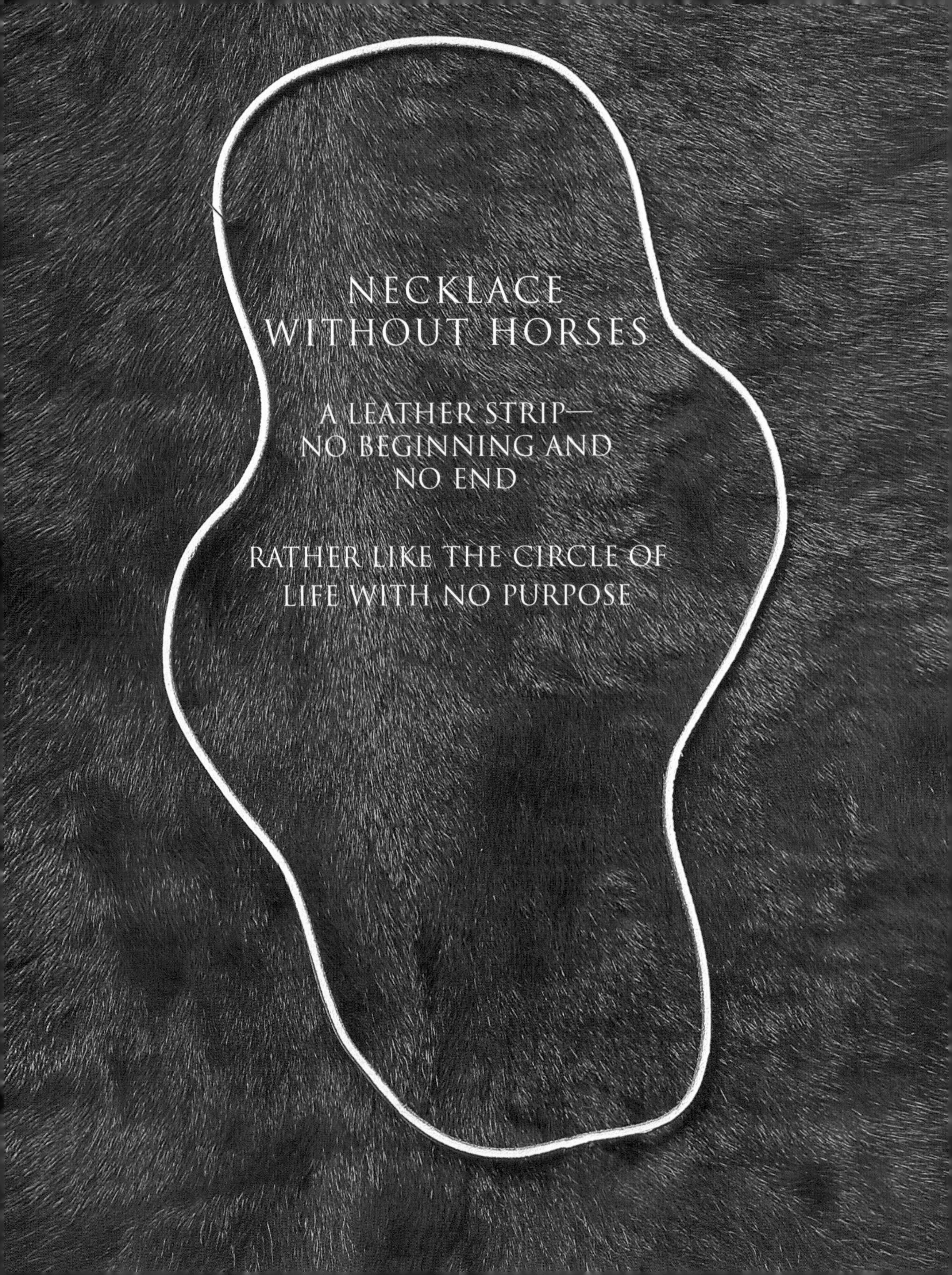

NECKLACE
WITHOUT HORSES

A LEATHER STRIP—
NO BEGINNING AND
NO END

RATHER LIKE THE CIRCLE OF
LIFE WITH NO PURPOSE

GINGER

I n the life of every horseman, there can be just one first horse. In my case, his name was Ginger. He was around thirteen years old when I met him, and I was two. I like to imagine our first meeting, myself an infant, not in any sense aware of what life had in store, while he was a true old professional. He was a retired ranch horse, a strawberry roan, born on the Uhl Ranch around 1924, and he had been shown in competition at ranch-hand gatherings in the late 1920s. God only knows what his breeding was. He appeared to be part Thoroughbred and part Spanish descent, but he had a little feather on his leg to suggest that maybe there was a draft horse somewhere in his family tree. He was about 15.2 hands in height and weighed around 1,150 pounds—he was no pony.

I don't have any memories of the start of our relationship—I was too young. But my mother told me that I rode Ginger by myself during my third year and I do have clear recollections of people exclaiming, "That boy is only three, and look at him ride!" Apparently, I was able to walk, trot and canter. I had every advantage—my parents lived and worked on the Salinas Rodeo Competition Grounds, which comprised over two hundred acres of land just outside the city of Salinas, California. This wasn't exactly a rural landscape, though; it was covered with buildings, all of them to do with

I won my first trophy on June 25, 1939, riding Ginger in the Junior Stock Horse Class. The prize was presented to me by actress Jane Withers.

horses. There was a full-size show ring with a grandstand for two thousand people, hundreds of box stalls, every size of corral and enclosure and a set of breeding barns. This land had been gifted to the city of Salinas on the condition that it be used as a riding facility by the townspeople. My family lived and worked at this establishment, training horses and running a riding school, so horses were part of our lives, twenty-four hours a day. It was in many ways perfect for a young child who liked horses, but it was also a lot of work and my father was a hard taskmaster. People had to be tough in those days. We were in the middle of the Great Depression and the Second World War was looming.

On June 15, 1939, when I was four, my father entered Ginger and me in a junior stock-horse competition in San Juan Bautista, a small community some twenty-five miles from Salinas. The other competitors ranged in age up to sixteen years. When it came to my turn, the judges asked me to complete an elementary reining course. Ginger and I did a couple of figures-of-eight complete with flying lead changes, cantered down to the end of the arena, stopped, settled and made the half-turn left. We cantered to the other end, stopped, settled and made the half-turn right. Then we cantered to the center, stopped and backed up eight to ten steps. When we left the arena I had a great big smile on my face, thinking I had done it all on my own. The truth was, of course, that Ginger had done it. We still have grainy film footage of Ginger executing those maneuvers and when I watch it now, I can see that I was just a passenger. Ginger did it all on his own.

We won the trophy, which was half as tall as me. Jane Withers, a child movie star of the time, presented it. She was always a lighthearted girl in her films, bringing laughter to everyone. Later, she became famous nationally as "Josephine the Plumber" in a long-running TV advertising campaign. Even today I can relive the intense excitement I felt back then as I accepted the trophy from her, and I still have it on a shelf at home. The brass work is a little tarnished and the joints are loose, so it doesn't stand quite straight anymore—a lot like me—but I treasure it, as you may imagine. The inscription reads: "Champion, Children's Division, M. Roberts, aged 4." Ginger's name isn't mentioned.

Ginger was more than my teacher; he also fulfilled the role of adoptive parent. Human infants are vulnerable. They need protection from the dangers of life, and parents are meant to be their protectors. They have a responsibility to feed and care for a child not yet capable of providing for itself. While my mother was both nurturing and protective, my father wasn't. He was cruel to me and I was afraid of him. I was to discover later, through my aunt Alice, his sister, that violence had been the order of the day in his own childhood.

I learned well before my third birthday how to escape from that cruelty—by running to Ginger. While I was riding Ginger, it seemed that my father couldn't catch me. Ginger's flying hooves took me away from the world of whips and beatings and the aggressive words that hurt more than any beating could, and in his stall I could hide with a friend who protected me and seemed to care for me.

With my mother's help, I even slept in his stall from time to time, when her body language somehow communicated to me that it would be better if I weren't in the house. My bed was in Ginger's hay manger, and I was kept warm by an old-fashioned canvas sleeping bag. I suppose, although I don't know, that she told my father I was somewhere else. I don't think he knew.

The Second World War changed everyone's lives. Ginger and I were no exception. A stranger turned up at the gates, wearing a business suit and carrying a briefcase—a rare event in itself. My brother, Larry, and I watched this man as he talked with my mother and father. They showed him around. He examined the box stalls and paid particular attention to the perimeter fencing. He completed measurements and made notes in a little book. At the ages of six and seven, Larry and I were old enough to know that something was going on.

It turned out that he was a representative of the United States government. A month later, a letter arrived informing us that the United States military was requisitioning the Salinas Rodeo Competition Grounds in order to convert it into an internment camp for Japanese-American citizens. We would have to move out immediately and, worse, my parents would be forced to get rid of forty to fifty horses.

This was bewildering. A whole section of the community—some of them our classmates—was to be imprisoned here, the stables converted into basic living accommodation. Soldiers with guns would be manning the gates. There was rationing of food, and some of my uncles were now in uniform and being sent to the far corners of the world.

Worse was to come. We had to shrink our operation dramatically and move into a rented house within the city of Salinas. There was no time, or resources to maintain all the horses. Gas was rationed, curtailing travel. Horsemeat was required to boost the war effort. Everyone was in a hurry.

A stream of vehicles turned up to collect our horses and ship them to a killing plant in Crows Landing, California. Unbeknownst to me, Ginger was among them. When they got there, they were unloaded and moved up a ramp with the aid of an electric prod. A steel door lifted and closed behind each one. Behind that door, Ginger was killed. Weeks later I learned of his fate.

I had been with Ginger for many hours, every day of my life, between 1937 and 1942. He was the cave I had hidden in for safety, he was the tree I had climbed to play, he was the blanket I had rolled myself up in for comfort, and he was my partner in winning my first trophy. Suddenly he was gone, and his fate was unthinkable. I felt betrayed by every human being in my life—by the American government, by the Japanese and especially by my parents. I cried uncontrollably, night after night. I tried to understand the complications of war, but no matter how hard I worked at it, I could never justify the death of this eighteen-year-old strawberry roan that had so much life left in him.

The loss of Ginger made me realize how valuable friendships are. He is naturally the first stone in my necklace. I don't remember the first time I rode him—he simply rises into my life. I loved Ginger as much as any child has ever loved his first horse.

BROWNIE

We moved out of our home on the Salinas Rodeo Competition Grounds and into the town itself. My father had a new job, as a policeman. We rented an old house at the corner of Church and San Luis, 347 Church Street. It was a three-bedroom, framed structure, costing $35 a month. In addition, my father rented a farmer's barn about two miles away on Villa Street, on the edge of town. It was there that we kept the few horses we could hold onto while awaiting our return to the real world of horsemanship. We had a stallion named Johnny Stewart, a mare called Babe and an offspring of hers sired by Johnny Stewart. There were a few others around that were owned by clients of my father.

We were at war. I remember my mother bringing a globe into my room and showing me the size of Japan and the size of the United States. She told me that this mess would be cleared up in a few months and we would be back on the Competition Grounds, living once more with our horses. She didn't show me Germany or Italy, and I really didn't know the extent of the world war until we had been in it for a year or so. I had four uncles in uniform, and I knew that one of them was in the South Pacific. The second was in the navy, the third was a pilot somewhere near India, and the fourth was in the infantry and fighting in Belgium. We wouldn't return to the Competition Grounds in a few months. The war kept us from our home until 1947.

In our old house I had grown used to hiding from my father, and under our new circumstances that hadn't changed. He worked shifts, choosing mostly to work at nights—the graveyard shift—and I was always busy checking my pocket watch, keeping tabs on where he was, when he'd be back, when he'd be gone. It hung from my belt on a leather thong, and it was in and out of my jeans twenty times a day. I still have that pocket watch. My grandfather gave it to me. It's silver, marked "Waltham," with Roman numerals, and railroad issue, so it's pretty much unbreakable. I give these details because it was the most important instrument to me at this time, telling me when my father would appear and when he'd have to leave. To this day, I'm told, I've got an obsessive relationship with time. I always know what time it is, give or take a minute or so.

With hindsight, I can see that my parents recognized the traumatic effect on me of Ginger's death and wanted to help me recover. My father began to introduce into his conversation a young brown mustang that he called Brownie, and my mother kept hinting that I needed a younger horse—why not Brownie?

Of course, I disliked Brownie. No one could—or should—replace Ginger. After a while, though, I realized I couldn't blame Brownie for something he knew nothing about. Only human beings could be blamed for what had happened. I began to take an interest in him.

Brownie was very much the classic cross between the Thoroughbred and the mustang. He stood about 15.1 hands and weighed approximately 1,050 pounds. Most of the pure mustangs were less than 14.2 hands and a large one might reach 1,100 pounds. Brownie had the head and neck of a typical Thoroughbred but was shorter, coupled with thicker conformation. He had the look of a quality horse with a finer coat and a more elegant neck and head presentation than any pure mustang that I have seen. He was a dark mahogany brown all over with a jet-black mane and tail and black points. He had a few white hairs between his eyes but you had to look hard to find them. He was probably bred as part of the remount project, which was an initiative conducted by the United States government to produce cavalry horses. It entailed releasing domestic stallions with mustang mares in order to achieve offspring that were larger than most mustangs and capable of being cavalry mounts. They even put some draft horses out there to produce offspring the size and strength necessary to pull the large cannons. Brownie's father was probably a Thoroughbred.

In my view, my father was just as cruel to Brownie as he was to me. In fact, my father was only using the standard methods of the time, and it's worth going into their background, particularly since these methods are still being used in many parts of the world.

When the Spaniards first came to what we now know as the United States, there were literally millions of buffalo, antelope and deer, but no horses—not one. The Spanish brought horses with them. Slowly, over time, some of these horses broke free, were let go or were stolen by the Indians. Despite a vast array of predators—mountain lions, wolves and bears are all able to bring down adult horses—some of them survived and began to breed. We've come to know them as mustangs, a word that comes from "mestengo," meaning "wild thing" in Spanish.

The method most pioneers knew of dealing with horses was the Spanish way, and the Spanish cowboys, or *vaqueros*, used incredibly harsh methods. It's no accident that the term "break" came to be accepted as a name for the process of subduing them. They broke the horses' will to fight, and they demanded obedience or they would cause great pain. One of the techniques involved tying up the horse's legs. The most common method was to truss one hind leg at a time to the neck and shoulders. The hind leg was held about a foot off the ground, which required the horse to stand on three legs. The idea was that the horse should fight against the rope until his will was broken—and then he'd stop fighting. This methodology kept going, down through the decades.

Sure enough, I watched my father employ similar methods with Brownie and the other horses in his care—it was nothing unusual. If Brownie shied at an object blowing across the path, my father would "sack him out," as it was known. Brownie hated this punishment more than any other. My father would place a large rope around his neck and then drop it through a heavy halter. Next he'd tie Brownie to a sturdy post, restraining him with unbreakable equipment. He'd use another heavy rope to force one hind leg off the ground so it became virtually impossible for Brownie to move without falling. He'd attach a large piece of canvas or similar scary object to a rope about thirty feet long. Then, standing twenty feet or so from Brownie, he would throw the frightening object at him. Brownie would panic and try to flee, resulting in his falling and often injuring himself. He would fight and fight against the ropes, but he could never win.

It was during one of these sessions that my father decided to use a crinkly type of crepe paper used to wrap lettuce in boxes. Salinas, being the lettuce capital of the world at the time, had an abundance of this paper. For Brownie, it made an awful sound that drove him out of his mind, and he remained frightened of the sound of paper until the day he died.

When I saw the brutal treatment Brownie received at the hands of my father and the pain he suffered, I felt a sense of kinship and began to grow attached to him. This created an additional responsibility on my part: I had to protect Brownie from my father. As a rule, my father slept from nine or ten in the morning until around three or four in the afternoon. With the help of my pocket watch, I could judge when he would be around and knew when to take Brownie to a back area and bit him up—a technique for leaving him to wander free with his tack on—so I could keep him from my father's sight. As soon as I was able to ride without my parents being worried that I might be injured, I was mostly left alone with Brownie. I'd ride him down the paths or in the fields on the edge of town, working with him and waiting for a time when he and I could go back safely.

I was escaping, and I was making sure, as much as possible, that Brownie escaped with me. We were in flight from pain and aggression, and that flight took us to some places that otherwise we would probably never have gone. One of these was a place everyone called "the willows," a lowlands marsh thickly covered in

Brownie and me on a practice day
at Villa Street Stable, 1945

willow trees about a mile and a half from the stables. I hacked out narrow paths through the branches, and Brownie and I could get lost in there for hours on end. If anything had ever happened to us, no one would have known, but I considered it a safer environment than the one at home.

Being on my own with Brownie accelerated my growing up and drove me to become a more effective horseman. I became responsible for some important duties beginning around the age of eight. I walked to the Villa Street barn and fed the horses before going to school. The Sacred Heart Grammar School was only about a mile from there. I left work clothes at the barn, as our school required a uniform. I could walk back after school, change and ride Brownie for hours on end.

My father had a full schedule and when he decided it wasn't necessary for him to school Brownie any longer, without a word being spoken Brownie became my horse. We worked hard and we practiced hard, Brownie and I. We weren't just running away now, we were running toward something as well—we were aiming for success in competition, once the war was over. Horse shows and rodeos had been suspended, but we could see the time coming when they would be revived. Competing was a way of preventing trouble with my father. Audiences would mean safety because violence toward me would not happen in public view. Horse competitions would provide a safe haven for Brownie and me, and the more successful we were in front of an audience, the safer we'd be. If Brownie and I could achieve good results in a show, it would reflect well on my parents' riding school, which would have to be started up again in earnest once the war was over.

Brownie was a talented horse and along with his ability came a forgiving attitude that I wasn't able to fully appreciate until much later in life. Somehow he was able to forgive the brutal treatment of his past and remain generous. During training he constantly amazed me with his cooperative and willing attitude. His one area of difficulty was with flying lead changes. But this shortcoming only served to make me a better teacher. I studied flying lead changes so much that they became one of my strongest talents as a trainer.

After the completion of flying lead changes in competition, the Western stock horse must execute fast runs culminating in sliding stops. Brownie was world-class at this maneuver. And he was extremely good at accomplishing spinning turns with the slightest of pressure on the reins. I made sure to keep on telling my father about Brownie's and my progress. If he hadn't heard about it, he'd have been on my case. He would probably have taken over Brownie's training program. At the same time, he greeted any success we had with criticism instead of approval, and I dare say this created an even stronger desire in me to win.

By the time we returned to the Competition Grounds in 1947, Brownie and I were a team. We'd had over four years to prepare and, believe you me, we were ready to compete. I was twelve and there simply was no other twelve-year-old in the United States able to take on Brownie and me. We won one championship after another.

We also practiced team roping together. In fact, he was the horse I learned to rope on. Although he was a better horse for heeling than for heading, he was good either way. After a partner roped the head of a running steer, Brownie and I would attempt to catch both hind legs, which is called heeling. This was, and still is, the method used on the ranches of the western United States to doctor cattle. If you find a sick or lame animal miles from any corral or holding facility, the best way to doctor it is to head and heel. The horses maintain the tension on the ropes to hold the animal while someone performs the necessary medical procedure. Brownie and I helped with the doctoring of a lot of cattle, mostly to administer medication for pinkeye. If one doesn't medicate early and regularly, the animal can lose the sight of the affected eye. Often in the spring we had to doctor for bloat, a problem that occurs when feed is plentiful. Cattle will blow up with gas and will die if you don't relieve them of the excess.

Brownie and I had a little game we played. I would put a steer in a square corral, and Brownie and I would stand in the middle of the corral while the steer inevitably found its way to a corner. We would allow the steer to turn, with its head toward us, and then we would run toward it at top speed. When the steer moved, Brownie would do an immediate U-turn, putting me in a position to rope the hind legs. This meant that no header was necessary, and the animal didn't have to be pulled for practice. Brownie seemed to love this game and became very proficient at it. I was able to rope for half an hour or more each day while never pulling the steer's legs or causing it any discomfort. Brownie would dance in place in a piaffe-like movement and then, with a subtle cue from me, he'd make his run. I suppose we practiced roping together more than anything else throughout the late forties. He taught me much about handling cattle from horseback and how to encourage horses to perform because they want to. We won many team roping events together.

Then there were the ever-present gymkhana events. Musical chairs, pole bending and races of every description were a vital part of the junior horse shows of the forties and the fifties; they were important in the total scheme of things. Each of the junior competitions offered a championship they called the All-Around. This went to the winner of the most accumulated points. The gymkhana events contributed the same number of points as the stock-horse class or Western equitation.

The All-Around at any given horse show would provide the winner with the largest and most prestigious trophy of the day, but more important, the points awarded went toward county, state and national championships. I was determined to win the All-Around at every gymkhana I entered. Brownie was absolutely incredible to ride in the musical chairs. You might think this is just a game of chance and that if you're near an empty chair when the music stops, you're in luck. This is not the case. Brownie knew how to stack the horses up behind him, cantering extremely slowly if he needed to, or running all out to stay in front of the competitors. No matter when the music stopped, Brownie left me with chairs available, and I recall winning something in the order of twenty-two straight musical-chairs events.

Brownie carried me a long, long way. Between 1947 and 1952, when I was twelve to seventeen years old, he and I traveled approximately 250,000 miles in trailers, trucks and even an old railroad car. Brownie accompanied me from the top to the bottom of California and ventured with me into Arizona, New Mexico, Nevada and even southeastern Oregon on one trip. Sure, there were other horses in my life during those years. I entered competitions for jumping and for gaited horses as well as those in the Western division. I rode dozens of other horses, including Mischief, Burgundy and an assortment of American Saddlebreds, but at this formative stage of my life, Brownie was my horse and he knew it. He was my favorite, sending me into the competition ring with more confidence than I had with any other horse.

We had great adventures outside of the arena as well, chasing wild cattle at night, in total darkness, on the Laguna Seca Ranch near Salinas. A lady called Dorothy Tavernetti paid us by the head. Brownie was an incredible partner in this task. We also spent weeks following mustangs, and he would assist me when we got home, working with the wild horses in the home corrals.

I had been competing on Brownie for four years or so when I noticed that his performances were tailing off a bit. No matter how hard I tried, we just seemed to be drifting downward in our scores. As it turned out, trying so hard was the cause of our problems. I wanted perfection every day of the week and I wasn't able to see or hear Brownie's side of the issue.

Professional trainers advised me that Brownie was jaded. He was becoming sour because of the grueling practice schedule that a young, enthusiastic rider was putting him through. He needed a rest.

I took the advice I was given and had a conversation with Brownie. Of course, the conversation was with myself really, but he was there and I talked to him as though he understood every word. "I'm going to ease up on our practice schedule, and if you'll promise to give me 100 percent on Saturday and Sunday, I'll allow those Tuesday, Wednesday and Thursday workouts to be much easier." Brownie didn't understand English but he certainly responded to the good advice given to me by those trainers. His performances immediately improved, and shortly after this decision we marked the high point of our career, winning the All-Around Championship at the largest junior Western competition in the United States.

I recall going back to Brownie's stall and thanking him (in English) for teaching me a good lesson. I made a pledge that I would listen to the signals he gave me, that I would try my hardest to know what he was thinking, to talk his language, if you will. Now I realize the importance of that place and time. Brownie made me want to learn about the psychological needs of horses. He was a wonderful teacher, counselor and motivator.

Brownie and I were approximately the same age—seventeen years old—when we rode down one day to play our game in the square corral with a steer. After seven or eight forays into the corner, we were standing in the center of the corral preparing for our next run. Nothing seemed out of the ordinary. Brownie was excited, as usual, and when the steer was right, he took me to the appropriate spot just as he always did. But as he made his turn to set me up for my throw, I felt an unusual movement. Brownie nearly came to a full halt, and then I felt him spread his legs and stagger. I recall looking down and wondering what was going on. Brownie leaped forward and crashed to the ground. I was thrown clear.

I got up, in a state of shock, and stood looking at Brownie. He was motionless. I don't know how I got to him, but I remember putting the back of my hand to his fore flank just under the cinch, trying to feel a heartbeat. I cupped my hands over his nose and begged him to breathe for me. I placed my palms on his side and pushed for many long minutes, hoping for a miracle.

It was no good. Brownie was dead. I stood up and watched as his eyes took on a silvery, opaque glaze. I felt the silence and emptiness of life without him.

No rendering plant was going to take Brownie. I was going to bury him where he died, right there on the Competition Grounds. I got some hand tools and began to dig a grave. I worked for several hours—the ground was as hard as concrete.

I vividly recall my father coming to me when he got the news. I suppose he understood the loss of a horse more than he understood any other of life's challenges. He put his hand on my shoulder and told me how sorry he was. He said he knew how much Brownie had meant to me. It was the only time he ever treated me with compassion. I had lost a friend but experienced the one single moment of kindness I was ever to receive from my father.

After ten minutes or so, he went to the house and made a telephone call to a man by the name of Kennedy who owned a construction company. He made arrangements for a mechanical digger to be brought to the site, so a proper grave could be dug for Brownie, a horse too wonderful for words.

In 1999, some forty-seven years after Brownie's death, I happened to be in Salinas when I was told they were tearing down the stalls on the old Competition Grounds. I went up there to have a last look and found that both Ginger's and Brownie's stalls were still standing—they had both lived at the north end of the barn and the wrecking machines hadn't quite reached that far. I approached the foreman and told him I had been raised there. Would he mind if I took a board or two from a couple of the stalls, as mementos? "Hell," he said, "I wish you'd turned up earlier. We've got to pay to haul this stuff away. Take what you want." I pulled off a board from Brownie's stall and one from Ginger's. I have them to this day, tucked out of sight so no one mistakes them for firewood.

Brownie's journey through life stopped that afternoon, but he started me off in the direction I've followed ever since. Brownie and I ran from aggression and violence. We ran as far and as hard as possible in order to escape, and in my work with horses, I've kept going the same way—away from aggression, pain and violence.

Even as I write this, I'm working with a horse that is phobically frightened of plastic shopping bags—just as Brownie was scared of that crinkled paper. With the approach I've used on this horse, after just two short sessions I can rub him all over with plastic bags. I rub his head and congratulate him as he allows the awful object into his life. Not one moment of pain was used in treating this troubled horse.

Brownie encouraged me to see the world through his eyes, to respect his needs and to realize that even our best friends will be less than perfect at times. Brownie needed me to protect him from the traditional world of harsh horsemanship. He was certainly one of the main reasons I've dedicated my life to nonviolent training. He was the perfect horse to become that stone in my necklace following Ginger. He was responsible for showing me that life is a two-way street: he received my protection and rewarded me with outstanding performances week after week. Brownie caused the horse world to think that I was a champion when all the time he was the champion, tugging the best out of me. The memory of Brownie will never wane so long as I live.

Today, as I sit signing autographs for people who come to my demonstrations, I often recognize that certain look in the eyes of a child who has a special horse at home. I know that look because I had it too. When I had Ginger and then Brownie, I also had a special horse at home.

MISCHIEF
AND DAN TACK

I first saw Mischief on the day she was born in the Villa Street barn. She was a dark brown filly, struggling to control her legs and take her first steps. The barn was my environment, my place. I was fourteen and had been mucking out, feeding and grooming there since the age of eight. Now the magic spell cast by the new foal aroused protective instincts in me. I felt almost as much responsibility for her as her own mother did.

I watched Mischief grow. She was strong and confident, enjoying the protection and nurturing that is the birthright of every infant. Yet with each inch she grew I felt more dread—when she reached her full height, just over 14 hands, she would be ready for breaking in. If the normal course of events was allowed to happen, her legs would be tied and she'd be sacked out until the fight was taken out of her. She would feel the full force of the world of human misunderstanding. I was determined to save her from that experience if I possibly could. I had managed to get Brownie out of my father's clutches sometime after he'd been subjected to the traditional methods of horse breaking. Maybe I could save Mischief from violence and pain right from the outset.

My father, who was still working in the police force, was preoccupied with that and with the newly restarted riding school back on the Competition Grounds. I maneuvered things so that he'd give me permission to start and train Mischief all on my own. He expected me to tie her legs and do the sacking out—he'd shown me how, many times. But I was determined not to use ropes, posts or whips.

My father had a predictable pattern. He'd be home from the night shift around seven in the morning, and I would make sure I was hard at work cleaning stalls because he'd launch himself into a kind of frenzy for an hour or two, to get the day up and running. He'd go to bed around nine and sleep until three or four. That was my window for training Mischief my way. I would patiently ask her for her cooperation and trust.

Mischief was accustomed to human handling and had a friendly disposition. It wasn't long before I was leaning my weight over her back, getting her used to it. I familiarized her with the saddle and bridle, allowing her all

Winning a hackamore competition on Mischief, 1949

the time she wanted. It wasn't such a big step for her when I suggested the saddle might rest on her back. She was wearing a halter and hadn't endured a moment's pain.

All this time I worked at keeping her away from the house and trained with as much privacy as possible. None of the brutality that I had observed in the traditional methods was necessary, not for one minute, not for any reason. My father's schedule worked to my advantage, and I believe that by the time he saw Mischief, she was doing well enough for him not to question how she was being trained. I remember him saying, "She's just a natural."

Mischief progressed through the first year of training exceptionally well. She was a willing worker and had none of the anxiety that traditional training often produced. Short and stocky as she was, it was not easy for her to express fluid athleticism. But I was pleased that she could accomplish flying changes better than Brownie—it gave me confidence that Brownie's difficulties with them were not entirely due to my inept training.

When I began to ride her, we had been back at the Competition Grounds for about a year. In July 1949, I entered Mischief in open competition—that's to say, against all comers, adults included—in the hackamore class. Introduced by the Spanish, the hackamore is a bitless rawhide noseband requiring a high degree of responsiveness from the horse to execute the maneuvers necessary for competition. We rode proudly into the ring and went through our paces, executing flying lead changes and doing our stops and turns. I felt the audience's eyes burning into me.

We won. I remember so well her picture on the cover of the local newspaper: a good advertisement for our riding school, so it kept us both safe from my father. By now, I knew better than to expect any praise or encouragement from him. It was a strange, contradictory feeling for me to win in open competition against adults, but to receive just a few surly criticisms from my father—that brought a mixture of triumph and disappointment.

Mischief was the first competition horse that I trained from the outset, and she proved that it wasn't necessary to be brutal to achieve top-class performances. I showed her only a dozen or so times, but she was part of my team in 1949.

Dan Tack carried me to the National Championship in Horsemastership, 1950.

Shortly after her picture appeared in the local paper, my father came to me with a proposal to sell Mischief. He'd had an offer of $2,000 from a lady by the name of Ruth Wilson. Mrs. Wilson would leave Mischief with us in training, which made it all the sweeter. He went on to say that I needed a better horse than Brownie or Mischief if I was going to go for the National Championship in Horsemastership.

A Texan was boarding horses with us for a short time, including a beautiful dun gelding called Dan Tack, by Arizona Dan out of a Hard Tack mare. These names are among the earliest registered Quarter Horses. If we sold Mischief, my father offered to buy Dan Tack. My mother and he were willing to put up the additional $500 needed. I thought Dan Tack was a beautiful horse with a lot of potential. He was larger than either Mischief or Brownie and of a higher quality of breeding and conformation. I had aspirations of winning a national championship, and it seemed to me that Dan Tack would make that possible. Everyone was waiting for my agreement and I felt involved in the deal. Money was changing hands, judgments were being passed, proposals made. I nodded my head and agreed to the sale. I was dealing in horses.

Dan Tack generously carried me to my first national championship, and it was through his efforts that I realized I had sufficient talent to compete at world-class level. His encouragement sent me forward in a way that might never have happened if he hadn't been in my life. A United States national championship is no small feat, no matter what the discipline, and I give Dan Tack a great deal of credit for that achievement.

Mischief stayed with us for many more years, becoming the riding horse for Ruth Wilson, who loved her and treated her well. Mischief was important in my life for two distinct reasons. The first is that she showed me that harsh treatment is simply not necessary to create a willing partner in a horse. The other is that she represented my first small step toward becoming a professional. She opened the door the first inch. Horses were not only to be my life and my passion; they were going to be my livelihood, too.

NO-NAME MUSTANG

I never knew the name of this horse. He didn't have one when I met him because he'd just been rounded up and brought down from the ranges of Nevada, and I have no idea where he wound up after the few days that I'm going to describe. Nonetheless, I have a crystal clear memory of what happened between us. It affected my entire life.

To try to explain what happened, I have to go back one year. In 1948, because of circumstances surrounding our return to the Competition Grounds, I was asked to go along with several adults to northern Nevada to assist in the yearly roundup of mustangs, which would be used in the wild-horse race in the Salinas Rodeo.

During the trip I developed a real enthusiasm for discovering how these vulnerable flight animals communicated with one another in the wild. Having read everything I could lay my hands on regarding the development of the horse, I was bubbling over with curiosity about how they survived in a harsh environment.

High up on the Nevada ranges, I found I could gain enough trust from family groups to allow me close enough to read their responses to one another through binoculars. I observed that they had a communication system, a silent one, made up of gestures rather than sounds. Silence was important if they were not to attract predators. The ear, the neck, the tongue, the shoulders and the tail of the horse were most often used to communicate with one another.

In particular, I noted the gestures used by the dominant mare to discipline the youngsters. The gestures were 100 percent predictable and measurable. If a youngster misbehaved, the dominant mare would drive him away, making him stand outside the herd, where he was in grave danger from predators. Only when the dominant mare received the correct signals of apology from him—his ear locking on to her, licking and chewing, and dropping his head low to the ground—would she allow him back into the safety of the group.

I also began to realize how important it was for horses to understand the gestures of predators. They read the feet of the cat and the shoulders of the bear just as readily as they read the gestures of the horses in their own family.

Fast-forward to the following year, 1949, and my second trip to the Nevada ranges. Having confirmed my observations from the previous year, I was eager to get home to see up close the mustangs we had captured. At the back of my mind was the idea of trying out these signals for myself. Would a mustang respond to me in the same way as I had seen them respond to their own kind? Could we exchange thoughts and signals? If so, we would have interspecies communication.

As I remember it, four of us returned home a day ahead of the mustangs with six domestic saddle horses. When we got back we slept for about fourteen hours straight. The mustangs—around 150 of them—arrived late the next afternoon and we spent the better part of two hours sorting them into pens, separating males and females. I believe we gave them about three days to eat, drink and rest.

Feeling as if I was the luckiest fourteen-year-old boy in history, I rode Brownie down to the corrals. I wanted to choose a subject and test my theories. These large corrals were divided into two columns of enclosures, separated by an alleyway about twelve feet wide and including a double-sized corral at both ends. Each had a large loading and unloading chute and a lane for entrance and exit. The fences were at least eight feet high and constructed of two-by-twelve-inch boards. Because the whole complex was painted dark green, it was referred to as the green corrals. I rode Brownie into the entrance/exit lane, tied his reins back to the saddle and began to walk between the corrals, looking at the mustangs left and right and watching out for injuries or illness.

I stopped at the gate of corral number two. The cowboys had allocated about ten young, healthy stallions to this enclosure, and as I stood there, my instincts tugged at me to go in and get closer to the small group.

How could life get any better than this? There I was, walking among these noble animals, the product of so many centuries of heroic survival. I don't think any horseman can walk through such a group without sorting them in his mind, scanning the herd in search of that outstanding individual. As the stallions looked me over with natural skepticism, a dark bay mustang caught my eye. I was inexplicably drawn to him as though we were magnetized. He didn't seem to be nearly as interested in me as I was in him; he was merely tolerant of my presence. This was my no-name mustang.

I zigzagged through the group eight or ten times, as I had seen the mustangs do, allowing my eyes to drift away from the dark bay stallion when he gave me his attention, but piercing his eyes with mine when he moved away. I was barely aware of the other horses in the pen. I felt a connection between us.

So far, so good. I had chosen the horse to work with but I wanted him on his own. I fetched Brownie and we filtered the other horses out until just the dark bay was left.

The next two hours must rank among the most important I've spent with any horse in my entire life. I walked into the corral and waited for the anxious, pacing young stallion to settle following the excitement of seeing his friends taken out. As I walked toward him, he began trotting or cantering

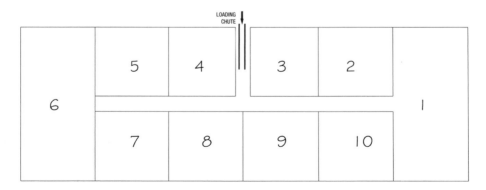

A diagram of the corrals where I worked with No-name and many other mustangs

around the outskirts of the enclosure, which measured about twenty yards square. Along one side, he had the comfort of seeing some other mustangs, a group of more senior males separated by a fence. Along this stretch, he focused on them. As he moved farther around, he was obliged to lose sight of them and instead began to concentrate on me. His ear locked on me. I knew that sign from my observations of his kin in the wild. It meant that he was according me the same respect as he would any predator, or indeed the matriarch of his family group.

The next time he went around, he found his friends over the fence again, and as he left them behind, his ear locked on me once more. Then he began a vigorous licking and chewing action with his mouth, and my heart practically stopped beating. This was an attempt to negotiate with me. I was sure it must be. It was the same signal that I had seen on many occasions in the wild. If so, it meant this mustang was asking me to show him I was not a threat—he was talking to me and I could understand.

Then, as he went around the fourth or fifth time, moving at a full trot, his head dropped until his nose was bouncing only inches from the ground. Any lingering doubts I had disappeared. There was no mistaking the gestures. I was witnessing the exact same combination of signals I had seen in the wild, in the same order and to an even greater degree than I had observed in Nevada. I was elated. My heart was practically bursting with excitement at what was going on here. At the same time I felt a flash of anger. I asked myself who was going to apologize to all the horses that had gone before for such utter and complete misunderstanding. It was clear now that horses enjoyed being our partners. They were willing to cooperate with us, if we would just communicate and request rather than demand.

After a few minutes, I wondered what would happen if I turned away from him and acted as I had seen the matriarch do when she received these same signals—give up eye contact and turn away.

The mustang stopped. I glanced over my shoulder. He was looking at me face on. I turned away and waited. A moment later, I became aware that he was walking toward me. No more than a yard away, he stopped. I was holding my breath, waiting for what would happen next. Would this wild horse attack me? No. I reached out to try to touch him but he moved off sharply. When I turned my back on him again, he came and stood at my shoulder. I took a pace or two and he followed. I kept going, my heart in my mouth, realizing that this mustang was following me, step for step. I stopped, he stopped.

I was exhilarated; my chest felt as if it were going to explode with excitement. I was communicating with a wild mustang. In showing him that I understood his language, I had gained his trust.

I wanted to tell my father what I had done, but I knew him to be prone to violence whenever I failed to follow his instructions to the letter. My mother was ever vigilant and quick to warn me when she sensed danger. In this case, I received that warning and realized that I could be heading for trouble. I knew by now that she was generally right and so I kept quiet.

I tried to tell my brother and various other trainers who were working their horses at the Competition Grounds at the time, but no one wanted to know. I couldn't believe it. Not one person took me seriously. It was a fake, a fraud, and it was dangerous, they said. I shouldn't be messing around like that or I would certainly end up dead, trampled under the hooves of a mustang.

I decided I had to keep this thing to myself until I thought someone would believe me. I didn't realize it would take forty years.

There's a strong case for this mustang being the most important horse in my life. There is just as strong a case for his being one of the most important horses that ever lived. His message would help the world to understand the language and the needs of these wonderful partners who share the earth with us. I have no idea what became of him. It's likely that he competed in the wild-horse race that year and was sold. He had virtually no value in the real world of the horse business, but the educational value he brought to me deserves a stone of major proportions in my necklace. I hope he had a good life with reasonable human beings.

BUSTER

The high desert ranges of Nevada create a unique landscape. The hills are stunningly beautiful, with variations in the thin soil making layered patterns. As far as the eye can see, deep barrancas, or small canyons, sprout stunted and tortured trees, and small scrub plants, primarily sage, grow everywhere. The night sky seems to go on forever, and the stars are so vivid I used to think I could reach out from my sleeping bag and pluck them with my fingertips. The thin air means freezing nights, but at sunup, the cold changes to warmth as if someone has flicked a switch. In summertime the heat can easily reach scorching levels.

In the summer of 1952 I was seventeen years old. Once again, I had the opportunity to take part in the mustang roundup, and, as usual, the Campbell Ranch supplied some Indian hands to help us. It was a yearly routine and everyone was well practiced and knew what to do.

On this trip I would have some spare days when I wouldn't have to be working, and I already knew what I would do with them. Over the last three years, since my encounter with the no-name mustang, I had been developing and practicing my ideas about communicating with horses. I called my system "join-up." I wanted to see if I could persuade a horse to accept his first saddle, bridle and rider while still in the wild. I wouldn't use a corral or pen of any kind. I would form a partnership with a wild horse on his home ground, using the technique that by now I knew wasn't a fluke or a fake. On the contrary, it worked every time. I would ride the wild mustang home—I was convinced I could do it.

I went scouting among the wild herds and eventually found a strong bay colt, probably four or five years old, showing a lot of Andalusian characteristics: high action in front, feathers on his fetlocks and a muscular neck and shoulder. He had large, black eyes with an excited glint to them. Horsemen might say he had an intelligent eye. His entire appearance appealed to me. He would be the one.

As I cut the young horse away from the herd, he was a magnificent sight. His neck was arched, his nose held high, and he stuck his tail straight up so that the hair flowed down over his hips. He ran as fast as he could and I followed, convinced I could persuade him to trust me and want to be near me. This would be the ultimate test of join-up.

The wild horse had a short, powerful stride, totally unlike that of the Thoroughbred. Working to bend him in different directions, I simply followed him, essentially driving him away. We soon settled into a zigzag pattern. I knew what to look for: the ear, the licking and chewing and the head dipping to a level near the ground. My experience at home with his brothers and sisters had taught me so much about interpreting the language of equus, as I had come to call it.

At home I used a circular corral about fifty feet in diameter with solid-wall fencing. It had no corners to interrupt the horse's flight and no outside distractions to claim his attention. The round pen concentrated the process. But here in Nevada there were hundreds of square miles of territory in every direction, with no fences of any kind. The mustang had no immediate need to negotiate with me. I needed patience. This process wasn't going to be measured in minutes, as it was at home. I kept on pushing him away, driving him out on his own, making him feel vulnerable enough to want to accept my company.

On the second day, it happened. He displayed those signals that told me he was asking to come in and talk to me. After some very patient negotiations, I could drop a rope around his proud neck and lead him around. He was still wild, but he seemed to be trying hard for me. Within another hour or so, I was dropping a long rope over his rear quarters and he kicked with purpose. When he kicked, I found myself saying, "Hey, Buster. What are you trying to do?" That's how he got his name, Buster. Soon the kicking subsided and I was able to advance to the next step.

I continued to progress—but very slowly, very calmly—through the procedures that I had developed with the mustangs back in Salinas. He gradually accepted the cinch, the long lines and then the saddle, with plenty of breaks in between for him to settle and get used to the idea of being in partnership with me. The first saddle I used on him was a Western saddle, and it seemed to be unacceptable. He kicked at the stirrups and bucked, but after a while his objections died down and he carried it with no great concern.

The following afternoon, I put one foot in the stirrup and gently lifted my weight onto it. I held the position and stroked his neck for a minute or so before easing my right foot to the ground again. I repeated the action a few times. Then I gave him a rest. After fifteen or twenty such repetitions, I leaned my hips well into the saddle and stayed up there. Buster moved a step at a time in a circular motion to the left, but he was calm and seemed ready to accept the idea of someone on his back. When the moment seemed right I slowly swung my right leg over his back and into the stirrup on the off side. I was riding him.

The area where I chose to try riding Buster was sandy, with no dangerous stones. I knew that if you were bucked off and injured out there by yourself, it could be life-threatening. I had a twenty-five-foot rope coiled in my belt and linked to Buster so that if he did buck me off I would have a chance of keeping hold of him. Horses have been lost in the wilderness with their saddles and, although I was convinced I could make him want to stay with me, I was still just a green kid.

Buster was by no means gentle but, like so many mustangs, he didn't want to buck. Wild horses try to conserve their energy and tend to buck only when they believe they're in great peril. Touchy at first, he would flinch and jump sideways with every movement of my hands or legs. Within twenty to thirty minutes, though, he settled. The next day, I rode Buster straight out and down the trail. In that huge landscape I felt as if we were the center of the universe. I rode Buster several different times that day, mounting and dismounting from either side.

On the morning of the fifth day, I began my trek back to the headquarters of the Campbell Ranch, where my adventure had begun. I rode my saddle horse most of the way to keep Buster fresh. Two miles from the ranch headquarters, and with no little sense of anticipation, I switched to

Buster. I rode him at a trot, leading my saddle horse and my packhorse. I felt a sweet sense of accomplishment as Buster marched into that barnyard as though he'd been doing it all his life.

A group of men were doctoring calves in a corral, some were working on a generator over by a barn, and others were coming out of the bunkhouse. They looked me over and asked what was going on. I told them what I'd done and expected to see their expressions change, to hear questions. Instead, I was received with disbelief.

"You must have taken an already broken horse and salted the herd," said one cowboy.

"Look at his feet," I countered. "He's never had a shoe on. You can see he's an out-and-out mustang."

"I can see he's been out there, all right," he said, "but you were lucky enough to find one that someone else has gotten to first."

This was the skepticism I had faced at home. "Here we go again," I thought, feeling angry and frustrated. I had achieved what I thought was a significant breakthrough in the way we dealt with horses and no one believed me. Maybe next year, I thought, when I had more experience, or when I had some kind of training establishment of my own. People would have to listen.

As I view it now, something spiritual was hard at work. Mother Nature had sent me the no-name mustang and then Buster and asked me to convince the world they could be dealt with in a nonviolent manner. Buster was unbelievably generous—he was willing to give up his freedom for a few days in an attempt to show me that I was on the right track. He worked hard to give me the evidence I needed to convince horsemen that violence is unnecessary. But once more I fell short at sending the message forward. Buster was only successful in validating these concepts for me. I released him back into the wild, but he sent me forward in life dedicated to leaving the world a better place for horses.

BERNIE

In 1955, when I was twenty, I was awarded a football scholarship to California Polytechnic University in San Luis Obispo. Just prior to entering Cal Poly, however, I injured my knee at the end of my two-season football career at Hartnell College, which ended my participation in the sport and meant I was unable to fulfill the obligations of the scholarship.

Although I enjoyed football, it wasn't the main reason I had chosen to go to Cal Poly anyway. It might seem odd to someone outside the western United States, but the college had a rich history in intercollegiate rodeo, just as some other colleges pride themselves on their football or rowing. I was asked to join the rodeo team's traveling squad immediately. From October to June I would be expected to compete in ten competitions in six states.

Rodeo evolved out of common work practices on ranches. Bulldogging, for instance, started as a competition between cowboys to see who could get to a steer the quickest when it broke from a herd. These cowboys had to hold cattle together in the open landscape, sometimes for many hours, and a steer breaking out caused great excitement. Everyone would try to get to it first, jump from his horse and throw the steer to the ground bare-handed. A black cowboy named Bill Pickett developed the trick of leaping from his horse's back in full flight and wrapping his arms around the steer's horns. He would then bite the animal's upper lip. This was how British

OVERLEAF *A rare photo of me bulldogging on Bernie in Phoenix, Arizona*

bulldogs brought down deer, so the event became known as bulldogging. Fortunately, the lip-biting part of it fell by the wayside.

Bulldogging, also known as steer wrestling, would be my main event. It's like performing a judo throw on a 700-pound steer while running full out. Many cowboys are injured while doing it, since the animals are much larger and stronger than any human. The steers typically weigh between 600 and 800 pounds and must have a mature set of horns. They are often imported from Mexico, where the sparse deserts produce animals with relatively small bodies and ample horn development. The primary cowboy has to ride past the left, or near, side of the running steer, stop it by leaping from his horse and grabbing his horns, and wrestle it to the ground with his bare hands. No ropes are involved. To prevent the steer from ducking away from the competitor, there is a second cowboy riding a horse on the right side of the steer, trying to keep the animal running in a straight line. The second-ary cowboy is called the hazer and his horse is referred to as a haze horse.

Team roping is also a skill that is used every day on ranches. One cow-boy ropes the steer's head while another ropes its heels to get the animal laid out for any veterinary treatment that might be necessary. With Brownie, I had helped doctor cattle many times. On a ranch, the work is done at a gentle pace and with minimum stress—no one wants injuries to animals or cowboys. In the rodeo arena, however, where the gloves come off, it's a timed event.

My first competition for the Cal Poly rodeo team would be in October in Eugene, Oregon. I needed a fast, responsive Quarter Horse, skilled enough in maneuvering for me to rope the rear legs of a galloping steer. Brownie had been my teacher in the art of roping, but he was gone now. Luckily for me, out of the blue came the answer to my prayers: Bernie.

Bernie was a little chestnut horse, originally from Arizona. He started out as my brother Larry's horse, but Larry joined the navy so Bernie was without a job to do. He'd originally been used as a heading horse, though he was only 14.3 hands and around 1,000 pounds. Roping the horns of a 600- to 700-pound steer and handling it so that the heeler can throw his rope is gener-ally reserved for horses closer to 16 hands and weighing over 1,200 pounds. With his lack of size, Bernie would have been hard pressed to excel at heading. But for heeling he fit the bill. He was short-coupled, nimble and fast, and he turned out to be a natural. His former life as a ranch horse had prepared him for the task, and I trained him for a short period of time as well. He was really eager. Even if the steer was swinging around on the end of the header's long rope, Bernie would chase that steer's tail and take every turn with my boot practically on the ground, he leaned in so far.

Bernie was also well suited for college rodeo because anyone could ride him. Since he'd been used as a heading horse, he was a useful backup for other members of the team should they need him, and he could assist in bulldogging as a primary horse or haze horse if required. In the language of professional rodeo, you'd call Bernie an all-around horse, which is exactly what team rodeo requires.

For four years Bernie was an ideal traveling partner—he was tolerant and made the best of situations that weren't always comfortable. I could leave him tied up to the side of the trailer while I made a few dollars, waiting at the bottom of icy roads to attach people's chains to their tires. Unlike other horses he didn't paw or call out. He'd always forgive my mistakes.

I remember one incident when Bernie probably saved my life and certainly prevented a severe case of frostbite. We were stranded together in an incredible snowstorm. His body warmth protected me while my teammate made a four-hour journey to buy a replacement tire for one that had blown on our trailer. I might not have had any hands afterward if Bernie's fore flanks hadn't kept them from freezing. As it was, I lost all the skin off my feet and ears in this near-death experience with nature.

Bernie stood by me and worked hard for me. Although it felt like I'd been married to him for four years, I was actually engaged to be married to Pat, and the date was set for June 16, 1956. As it turned out, the finals of the National Intercollegiate Rodeo Championships in Colorado Springs had been set for the same day. As the college year progressed and we participated in one competition after another, I was finding myself in a dangerous predicament. Bernie and I were accumulating enough points to qualify for the finals. It looked as if we had a chance of winning the World Championship in Team Roping. Should I choose Bernie and the rodeo team or Pat and my future with her?

As Bernie and I traveled around the western United States, I decided to set up a little joke on my future in-laws. At every stop for six months, I bought a postcard, wrote a note and addressed it. I planned to have some-body mail one card at a time to my mother-in-law while Pat and I were on honeymoon. She would receive a postcard every five days or so from a string of towns and read all about the classy hotels we were supposedly staying at. I knew Pat's mother was concerned about her beautiful daughter marrying a cowboy with limited (no) funds, and I thought the postcards would give her great joy—I was right. When Pat and I got back, we explained the joke and let her know that we'd been staying in a little cabin on the beach at Carmel, just twenty or so miles from Salinas. She took it well and laughed along with everyone else.

The team and the school were disappointed when I decided against making the trip to Colorado and to marry Pat instead but, on the other hand, they were happy for us. I made the right choice. Pat and I have three grown children, Deborah, Laurel and Marty, and three grandchildren, Matthew, Adam and Loren. Pat has been more than a good wife to me, bet-ter than I could have imagined. We met when we were eight years old at the Sacred Heart Grammar School, and we've been married now for forty-nine years.

Bernie made the trip to the championships, however, and assisted the team in acquiring a significant number of points. As it turned out, I had accumulated enough wins to nail down the championship without even attending the finals. Greg Ward, a teammate, rode Bernie into the arena to accept my saddle and trophy buckle. In front of the audience, he told the announcer that Bernie was the horse with which I had earned the qual-ifying points, and since he was the only reason I had won anyway, they were honoring the right individual.

Bernie was, indeed, a big part of my individual rodeo successes at Cal Poly, assisting me in earning my first national championship, and he was an even bigger part of the achievements of the team overall. He was just a little Arizona chestnut with an unknown sire or dam, and he'll never be remembered as a major rodeo star, but that doesn't matter. Bernie helped many young people to become better competitors. For me, he was more than a horse I rode; he was a good friend.

MISS TWIST

Miss Twist came into our lives around 1949 or '50, and blinding speed was the centerpiece of her existence. While throttle control was in short supply with Miss Twist, her ability to transport a rider for a hundred yards or so was incredible—riding her was like sitting on a rocket.

Miss Twist was by Hard Twist, one of the earliest sires in the Quarter Horse breed. Her mother was of Hancock breeding from the G-Fern Ranch. Initially, my father bought her to send her to the racetrack. In the western United States, there are regulation tracks for Quarter Horse racing, and Miss Twist was pretty much the quickest vehicle on the face of the earth for the first 220 yards. After that, she ran out of steam and slowed dramatically. Most Quarter Horse races ask for 350 yards.

Miss Twist came home from the racetrack at about the time I was going off to Cal Poly, and my father asked me to take her with me and train her as a bulldogging horse. In bulldogging, the horse has to be fast for only a maximum of a hundred yards and most efforts require less than fifty yards of full speed. Miss Twist should have been perfect, but she would certainly require careful training and skilled horsemanship.

When I began training her, she quickly drew the attention of every potential bulldogger at Cal Poly. Unfortunately, though, Miss Twist was not a particularly good horse for a college rodeo team. She wasn't user-friendly. Once the rider said go, Miss Twist went on autopilot. There was no adjusting speed or using good judgment for difficult surfaces or other environmental circumstances. She just went all out. Although she delivered me to many steers in the three- and four-second range, allowing me to win one bull-dogging event after another, most of my teammates were not specialists, and Miss Twist was not the horse for inexperienced cowboys trying their hand at bulldogging in pursuit of a few extra points.

Jack Roddy, who would go on to become a world champion bulldogger and a member of the Rodeo Hall of Fame, rode Miss Twist while on the team with me. I don't think he was ever very happy riding something like a runaway train past a slow-moving bovine whose horns he was expected to grab as he zoomed by. If you weren't ready for her seemingly uncontrollable speed, it was hard to concentrate on your bulldogging effort.

John W. Jones is said by many to be the greatest bulldogger who ever lived. Also a world champion and member of the Rodeo Hall of Fame, John has been the inspiration for many young bulldoggers, including his son, John Jr., who has won the world championship three times. John Sr. rode

Miss Twist several times at practice and professional rodeos, and I must say he made a gallant effort to get used to her. Still, he nicknamed her "Misfit," and the name stuck for the rest of her career.

The most memorable day in the life I lived with Miss Twist came when John W. and I decided to go to San Jose, California, to practice for a day or so on Jack Roddy's ranch. With us was Everett Muzio Jr., known by his friends as Junior Muzio. It was time to introduce him to Miss Twist.

John W. put Junior on Miss Twist, made sure his stirrups were right and gave him a few words of advice.

"When you ask her to go, she goes," warned John. "Be ready and quick to jump the steer. Don't ride her by your steer without jumping because

This photo shows Miss Twist outrunning the haze horse—the left stirrup was snapped away so fast it is over her back. Note my hat has been left hanging well behind. We won this one in Pomeroy, Washington, in 1955.

she will take you to the other end of the arena, and it will be a trip you'll never forget.

Well, you can guess what happened. Junior backed into the bulldogger's starting box and nodded his head, and Miss Twist took off from a standing start to full speed in about three strides. Junior went by the steer so fast that he hadn't even begun to prepare to jump. He sat up straight in the saddle and Miss Twist took him to the end of the arena, about a hundred yards away. Approaching the fence, Miss Twist made a hard left and leaned like a Harley-Davidson, making tracks two or three feet below and on the other side of the fence that she managed not to crash through.

Junior's face was as white as snow when he got back to the starting area, and he vowed never to make that trip again. I ran a few steers on Miss Twist, and because I knew her so well, I was able to catch them with very little difficulty. Meanwhile, John W. and Jack Roddy were both laughing at Junior and giving him a rough time. Half an hour later, they'd convinced Junior to try another trip on Miss Twist.

"You see how easy it is for Monty," John said. "Just jump. Don't ride by."

Trying to keep his male pride intact, Junior backed Miss Twist into the starting box again. After a second or so, he nodded his head and left the same way he had the first time. As he approached the steer at full speed, he lowered himself about half the distance to the steer's back, but it was too late—he found himself with nothing but that fence staring at him from the far end of the arena. He straightened himself in the saddle and, being the good Catholic that he was, made the sign of the cross and bailed out. Junior tumbled for about twenty yards, scraping his elbows and knees and blackening one eye. He got up in a cloud of dust and said, "I like that a lot better." John W., Jack Roddy and I couldn't stop laughing for half an hour.

One time, the Cal Poly track coach invited an Olympic sprinter to be the guest of honor at a meet he was organizing. My rodeo coach, Bill Gibford, decided to race Miss Twist against the Olympic sprinter. I don't know what the human athlete was thinking when I rode Miss Twist, who was carrying 220 pounds of rider plus about 40 pounds of tack, and beat him by about twenty yards in a fifty-yard race.

Miss Twist allowed me to win bulldogging competitions almost every weekend throughout the 1956–57 rodeo season. I went to the national finals, once more held in Colorado Springs, in June of 1957 and successfully completed my quest to be the National Intercollegiate Rodeo Champion in Bulldogging. Miss Twist accompanied me into the arena to receive the championship saddle and a silver and gold belt buckle. While most of my teammates could not figure out how I had ever learned to manage her blinding speed, they all realized that she was the key difference between the rest of the bulldoggers and me.

UP, PRINCE

By the fall of 1957, Pat and I had a six-month-old daughter, Deborah Gail. It was time to get down to the serious business of earning enough money to provide for a wife and family. We were living in an old railroad car that I had converted into basic living accommodation on a ranch near the Cal Poly campus. The arrangement allowed me to use the modest facilities there, and Pat and I told everyone in the community that we were in the business of training horses. If I remember correctly, I proposed that my fee for each horse would be $125 per month, including feed and stabling. We settled down to wait and see what would come our way.

One day, Pat's mother, Marge, came to visit and told me that our old-fashioned, wringer-style washing machine was just not adequate now that we had a baby. This was well before the advent of disposable diapers. An automatic machine would be far less work for Pat. Marge showed me an ad in the local newspaper: an automatic washing machine from Sears, Roebuck and Co. would cost us $160. I could put $20 down and pay just $10 a month for two years. Off I went with the ad clipped from the paper.

At the store, I was directed to the credit department to have my contract drawn up. But after I had filled out some forms, the lady behind the counter told me I couldn't buy the machine because I had never bought anything on credit before, and therefore had no credit rating. I would have to go home to Pat and her mother and tell them we'd have to carry on using the old wringer washer.

As I was about to leave with my tail firmly between my legs, I heard my name called out. "Are you Monty Roberts?" asked a young man who turned out to be a cousin of mine. I had many relatives in the San Luis Obispo area because my mother's family had homesteaded near there. I noticed he was wearing a Sears uniform, and he told me he was a maintenance man and also made deliveries. I mentioned my problem with the credit department and he ushered me back to the lady at the desk.

He told her I was a relative and that I was good for my payments. She said that if he was so certain, he'd have no problem cosigning the agreement and acting as guarantor—and that's what he did. I don't remember ever seeing him again. Now that I had to keep paying for that washing machine, I really needed some customers.

I came home one evening, tired from a long day of university classes and training horses, and Pat told me we had received a call from a lady in Baywood Park. She had a horse she wanted us to train but no trailer. Pat volunteered us to transport the horse and arranged a time to meet. Off we went, traveling west toward the Pacific Ocean.

Baywood Park is a beautiful seaside community about fourteen miles west of San Luis Obispo. The houses there each had about half an acre of land, which allowed for a large garden at the back or, as in this case, a small field with a one-horse stable. We parked our car and two-horse trailer in front of the house and walked up the path. Suddenly, a large side door opened to reveal a two-car garage with everything in it but cars. There were rabbit hutches and nesting boxes. There was hay, grain, a saddle, halters and assorted horse equipment.

Standing in the doorway was a friendly, middle-aged lady. She must have had to make more trips to the feed store than to the supermarket. Asking us to ignore the mess, she escorted us through the garage and out onto the lawn behind the house.

About twenty yards away we could see our new customer in his field. The lady said his name was Prince. He was a three-year-old half Thoroughbred stallion, nearly 16 hands in height. He was a bright bay and appeared to be healthy and athletic. The lady said she had a job and just didn't have time to train Prince herself. Apparently she'd raised her family and was now returning to riding after a long break. She'd ridden a lot as a youngster and felt she'd be fine if I could just give her horse one month of training.

As the three of us crossed the lawn, I suddenly noticed something too frightening for words. A smooth one-wire fence was stretched very tight just about waist high to form the boundary between the lawn and the field, and Prince was standing with one front foot outside the field and one front foot inside. The wire was between his legs, drawn up tight into his chest area. This was a chilling sight. Virtually every horseman has seen horses seriously injured by wire fences, which can cut like a knife.

I took the lady's arm and reached out for Pat, too.

"Wait a minute," I said. "Stop. We've got a problem here. The horse is tangled in that fence."

"Oh, no," the lady said. "He does that all the time. He's just waiting for my husband to come and feed him."

"If he does this all the time," I asked her, "how the heck do you get him off the fence?"

"No problem," she replied, handing me a lead rope. "You just snap this into the halter, back up to the end of the lead, lift both of your hands in the air and yell, '*Up, Prince!*'"

I stared at her. What kind of circus was this? I looked over at Pat, who simply buried her mouth in her hands and doubled over, fighting back laughter. Here I was, National Champion in Horsemastership 1950, National Champion in Team Roping 1956 and National Champion in Bulldogging 1957, and this lady was asking me to stand at the end of a lead rope, lift my arms and yell, "Up, Prince!"

Pat rolled her eyes and said, "Monty, if it works, do it." My inclination was to run like a rabbit, get in the car and drive home. But I had those payments to make, and I couldn't let my cousin down when he'd been so nice as to guarantee I was creditworthy.

I walked very slowly toward the big horse. "Hello, boy," I said, soothing him. He stood like a statue but didn't look too pleased to see a total stranger interfering with his feed time. I had no idea which way he'd jump, but I snapped the lead rope to the bottom ring on his halter, backed up to the end and looked over at Pat, who just shrugged as if to say, "It's up to you."

I thought, "Well, in this instance, do as you're told and do it exactly as she said." I raised both my arms and yelled, *"Up, Prince!"*

Would you believe it, this horse—who had never seen me before in his life—stood straight on his hind legs, lifted himself off the fence and gently lowered his forefeet back into his field. It was incredible.

We loaded him into our trailer and headed home. I got my $125, Pat got to keep the washing machine, the mystery cousin was never called on to repay my debt, and Pat and I learned something from a three-year-old colt from Baywood Park, California. We learned that asking for something that seems impossible can sometimes result in success.

Pat promised she'd never tell anybody about this embarrassing first challenge for a new horse trainer, but I believe it was just three days later, over dinner with our best friends, John W. and JoAnn Jones, that she spilled the whole story. Telling John W. a story like that was certain to get it more exposure than reporting it to *The New York Times* would. From then on, if I was competing in a horse show or a rodeo, I'd often hear someone call out, "Up, Prince!"

I've always known that humility is a great virtue, but how much humility could one horse trainer bear?

RONTEZA

In late 1959, Sheila Varian came to San Luis Obispo with a young Arab filly she called Ronteza. Although Sheila was an accomplished rider, she wanted me to help her work on her skills in training and showing Western horses in competition. Sheila, only in her mid-twenties, was already a breeder of Arab horses and had a strong reputation for producing champions. In subsequent years, she has gone on to be one of the most successful Arab breeders in the world.

Ronteza was in the early stages of training when Sheila brought her to the farm, and she felt it was time to start her with cattle. Sheila was convinced that she had a champion working cow horse in this little bay mare. Ronteza had big, bright eyes that glinted with intelligence. Her ability to learn was more acute than that of any horse I had worked with to that point. She would watch me and then complete the task I had requested of her with unbelievable dexterity. At the time, I had about twenty Quarter Horses in training, and I would guess that ten or twelve of them were well into the cattle-working stage. Within ten days or so, Ronteza was passing my Quarter Horses as if they were wearing hobbles. She learned more in a day than most of the others were learning in a week.

I told Sheila that she should not be the one to show the mare. Ronteza was just too talented for a young woman with limited experience in showing working cow horses. I thought the filly could go on to be a real contender in world-class competition with all breeds, even though Arabs were not thought capable of accomplishing anything like this.

Sheila had quite another idea. At first she ignored me when I insisted I should be the one to show the horse, and later she became adamant that she and no one else would show Ronteza. At the time, I thought it a terrible shame that this talented young horse would remain unknown because of an inexperienced rider.

The cattle-working stage of Ronteza's training progressed unbelievably well and, with Sheila in the saddle, they won several major competitions the following summer in the hackamore division of the National Reined Cow Horse Association. I had to come to grips with the fact that, while I always preached to my students that they should never underestimate the potential of their horses, I was underestimating the potential of my human student.

Watching Sheila show Ronteza was an incredible source of pride for me, a double whammy if you will. Two students winning in the same class—what a feeling! Sheila and Ronteza served notice to the world of Western competition that they were ready to take on all comers, even if the filly's papers said "Arab" and not "Quarter Horse."

In November 1962, Sheila and Ronteza entered the National Championships to be held in the Cow Palace in San Francisco. This competition was the largest and most important of the National Reined Cow Horse Association—fifteen to twenty thousand spectators would attend each day. Sheila must have realized that her chances of beating the world's best on a 14.2-hands full Arab mare were slight, but you wouldn't have known it to look at her. She beamed with confidence throughout all three phases of the competition, and when it was over, Ronteza was the national champion.

All the big names of the day had been in there, competing with her—Don Dodge, Ray Hackworth, Bobby Ingersoll, Ronnie Richards, Greg Ward and I. I think I won third on a big strong Quarter Horse. But a tiny bay Arab mare ridden by a girl beat all of us.

The list of lessons taught me by Ronteza and Sheila Varian is as long as my arm. They demonstrated that the widely held belief that an Arab wasn't capable of winning a world-class reined cow horse competition was false. I

MY BLUE HEAVEN

Sometime during 1960 I got a telephone call from Joe Gray, a contractor from Santa Maria, California. Mr. Gray's gray mare, My Blue Heaven, was causing him some problems.

I already knew about My Blue Heaven because I had seen each of Mr. Gray's two daughters riding her in several shows. It was clear to me that the horse was becoming progressively more difficult to stop. When running at speed with the excitement of competition, she would lock her teeth on the bit and take the rider on a frightening trip. One of the primary objectives in Western competition is to get the horse to stop immediately by sliding the two hind feet, a maneuver that should be accomplished with minimum pressure on the mouth. Obviously, something had gone wrong with My Blue Heaven.

Mr. Gray told me that he was concerned for the safety of his daughters and felt the only solution was to sell the horse. But this was going to be a problem because, while the girls were having trouble stopping her, they were still attached to the mare. Mr. Gray and his family were about to go on a three-week vacation to Shasta Lake, California, and he wanted me to see the horse before they returned. He said he'd take care of the ensuing trauma and asked me to be on the lookout for a horse for each of his daughters that would be more effective in the show ring, and certainly less dangerous.

My Blue Heaven arrived the next day and with her came a note from Mr. Gray, repeating his instructions that the mare be sold within the next three weeks, no matter what the price. He would check in with me when he returned, at which time he'd assess any horses I might have chosen for the girls.

I rode My Blue Heaven that same afternoon and was surprised at how good a mare she was. Her spins, figure eights and cow work were world-class. I decided to try a stop.

I went very gently, asking her to stop from a trot in order to get an idea of what was troubling her. She immediately resisted the bit. She resented it and reacted badly to any pressure on her mouth, pushing into the bit with great force and refusing to stop. I remembered that she'd been ridden

My Blue Heaven, with me up, winning one of her many championships on the way to two reserve world titles in the Working Cow Horse division in 1960

with some very severe bits and pulled on heavily in an attempt to make her slide.

I decided to use the join-up technique with her, since it had proved to be an effective way of communicating with a horse, no matter the age or circumstances. I put My Blue Heaven in the round pen, which was out back and well out of sight of curious onlookers, so I could go through the procedure without being observed. I was still very concerned that my approach would meet with skepticism. Sure enough, the technique worked. A sense of trust began to build between us, layer on layer, session after session. I felt we were on the same wavelength. After about an hour, I was able to let her know that I understood what she was saying to me. She did not want to be forced to stop. I would have to create in her a desire to stop. For all intents and purposes, I'd have to start from the beginning.

I made sure I trained on the best of footing—not too hard, not too soft. At one end of my arena I had a wall around eight feet high and fifteen feet wide, made out of plywood and well braced. To begin with, I just trotted her around, so she'd be comfortable with this construction. Once she was used to it, I'd walk or trot her slowly up to the board, and just before her nose touched it, I'd sit down in the saddle and press down in the stirrups, giving the command "Whoa." I put no pressure on her mouth.

Maybe fifty times we trickled up to that wall in this manner, and at the first positive sign that she was reading my signals—the weight down in the saddle and stirrups, and the command—I quit. I dismounted and led her back to the stable, making her feel rewarded.

The next day, as we approached the wall for about the twentieth time, I asked her to stop fifteen feet in front of it without any pressure on her mouth. When she stopped, I got off, walked around and allowed her adrenaline to drop to a lower level, building an atmosphere of reward. On the third day, I asked for a little more, a little quicker. Within a week her behavior had changed. It seemed this beautiful gray Quarter Horse mare was learning how to have fun with her stops and no longer viewing them as a painful fight with the bit.

I was excited by her progress and toward the end of her second week, I decided to enter her in a forthcoming horse show at the Alisal Guest Ranch in the Santa Ynez Valley, about an hour's drive away. I was unable to reach Mr. Gray to get his permission, so I covered the $50 entry fee myself. Should My Blue Heaven put in a good performance, it was quite possible I would find a buyer at the competition.

With another week of schooling, My Blue Heaven got better and better. She reached a point where I thought she might win a ribbon at the horse show. First prize was a Jedlicka saddle plus some money, and while she couldn't be expected to win outright, that saddle was dangling there as the ultimate prize. At today's prices, it would probably be worth around $6,000 or $7,000.

There were close to twenty good horses in the competition and hundreds of people in the audience. Before the show started, I let it be known that My Blue Heaven was for sale. No one was interested.

I felt confident as our time came to perform. I believed in My Blue Heaven and she didn't let me down. Her figure eights with flying lead changes were virtually perfect. The next maneuver was the stop—My Blue Heaven would have to gallop at top speed down the middle of the arena and come to a sliding stop at the far end. To this day I can remember the feeling of exhilaration that came over me as I felt her hind feet scrape the ground with that awesome sound of a good sliding stop. Her spins were fantastic and her overall score had her near the top of the heap.

With the cow work left to do, excitement, fear and trepidation all rolled into a big ball right in the middle of my stomach. If we drew a good cow, we could possibly win the competition. The instant our cow stepped into the arena, I knew our chances were very good. We had drawn a tailor-made bovine, and My Blue Heaven's cattle score was outstanding. As we finished I recall looking toward the judge, Bill Gibford, my old rodeo coach. He was motionless, mouth agape. Mr. Gibford had seen My Blue Heaven many times, and he told me later that he never dreamed it possible for her to accomplish the level of work she turned in.

All the competitors rode to the center of the arena, and when our number was called to receive the first prize, my family and half the people there fell over in surprise. My Blue Heaven and I made a victory lap around the arena with the new saddle up behind me, and it was one of the most gratifying moments of my young career. You can imagine how many people met me at the back gate to ask what the price of this mare was and could they take her home with them then and there. I was pleased to say that, under the circumstances, I couldn't personally agree to any sale.

The next day I drove to Santa Maria with the saddle in my car. Though the Grays hadn't yet returned home, I had made arrangements with the lady who was looking after their house while they were on vacation, watering the plants and feeding the dogs. I placed the saddle in the dining room with a note attached: "Please be advised that My Blue Heaven won the Open Reined Cow Horse competition at the Alisal Guest Ranch show. This saddle was the trophy offered as first prize. Should you still be interested in selling her, there are a lot of potential buyers out there, but I think we should discuss this matter further."

The Grays arrived home about twenty-four hours after I delivered the saddle and called immediately. I'll remember that call forever. My Blue Heaven wasn't sold and she went on to enjoy many triumphs. Under my training, she was second for two years running for the World Championship in the reined cow horse division.

I was so fortunate to have that blue-gray mare in my life. She helped put me on the map in professional competition, and she reinforced what I already knew: force and demand are seldom the answer to achieving our goals with horses. She made me realize that if I could create an environment where the work was fun, the horse would be more effective.

My Blue Heaven stayed with the Grays until she died in the 1980s. She was buried on their property in Santa Maria.

HEY SAM

In 1961 I was in Oahu, Hawaii, judging a horse show on the windward side of the island. At the end of the day, Pat and I were invited to dinner at the beautiful home of Robert Anderson and his wife, Frankie.

Mr. Anderson told us about his two-year-old Thoroughbred colt, Hey Sam, and asked if we'd like to see him. Pat and I said we would, thinking we'd go out to the stables. Instead, the doors opened and Hey Sam was brought inside the house, there and then. You can imagine our surprise and delight at having a horse come right into the dining room. His beautiful bay coat shone and his manners were impeccable, a measure of how gentle he was. The Andersons said they had purchased him from the Parker Ranch on the big island of Hawaii. Their dream was to become successful racehorse owners and Hey Sam was their first purchase.

We agreed that he would come to me for pre-track training in San Luis Obispo, and I was very excited. I had always wanted to be involved in different disciplines of equine competition, and if I could start this colt successfully, it might open the door to the world of Thoroughbred racing, a long-held ambition of mine.

When Hey Sam arrived it was clear he'd been properly raised. He was well developed and healthy, and his handling had made him friendly, cooperative and generous. We were able to start working right away. Join-up was as effective as always at starting a relationship of trust and good communication. He completed his pre-track training in six months without incident.

"H E Y   S A M"
GOLDEN GATE FIELDS   4/19/65   DONALD ROSS   UP
SCRUB 2nd (2nd)   SIX FURLONGS   1:11;3   POOL HALL BILL (3rd)
ROBERT A ANDERSON JR   OWNER   FARRELL W JONES   TRAINER

Mr. Anderson selected a particular trainer at Hollywood Park, a major Thoroughbred racetrack in Inglewood, California, so that Hey Sam might proceed with his timed works. It wasn't long, however, before I received a call from the trainer saying that they were having a problem with Hey Sam. It seemed that his daily exercise rider had fallen into the habit of stopping him at the same spot on the racetrack after each training session. This spot was where two gates led off the track to the stables, which were obscured behind a high hedge. Hey Sam quickly realized that he could go back to the stables from there, and every time he approached the spot, he began to stop on his own and veer off toward the hedge.

Without the trainer present, the rider began to whip Hey Sam as punishment for his behavior. The horse grew resentful and refused to cooperate with the rider. The battle lines were drawn. Hey Sam became violent. Very soon the rider couldn't get Hey Sam past that point. As the rider and young horse approached the hedge, Hey Sam would bolt outward and stop abruptly against the hedge, trembling, and then he'd kick and fight if the rider so much as moved the whip. He would often stand on his hind legs, trying to unseat the rider as he fought any attempt to move him forward. An official report was lodged regarding his behavior, and Hey Sam was banned from all California racecourses.

I went to Hollywood Park and personally saw Hey Sam fighting his rider. There and then, I became an advocate for banning whips in racing. I've given demonstrations and made speeches around the world on how destructive the whip is. Movements to ban it are growing in Scandinavia and, to an extent, in England and western Europe, but the horse community in the United States has essentially turned a deaf ear, even to the idea of reducing the use of whips.

Watching Hey Sam was devastating for me. He had been such a gentle horse, a welcome guest in his owner's dining room back in Hawaii. I remembered the many horses who'd taught me that pain and pressure were never the answer in getting a horse to cooperate. I brought Hey Sam back to our farm and went to work to regain his respect.

Secretly, as always, I went back to the beginning to recreate a partnership of trust. The two of us spent many long sessions together for about six

Hey Sam's first race—what a day of joy

months. During that time I made sure he felt absolutely no pain. I rewarded him whenever he expressed the slightest generosity by stopping and stroking him till he felt relaxed and comfortable. Gradually Hey Sam became more and more generous.

It's my belief that a horse is never born bad. Hey Sam had no evil in him. He had been misunderstood and mishandled. Once I had finished work with him, I recommended he be sent back to Hollywood Park but this time to Farrell W. Jones, a champion trainer many times over. I rode Hey Sam for Farrell the first time he went out on the track, and as we came round the bend, that hedge loomed up. He went past without breaking stride or altering direction. He didn't even flinch. I felt elated as he continued to be cooperative while we tested his reaction to that dreaded spot.

Though the racing stewards were still concerned about Hey Sam, they seemed to be satisfied that my work on the farm had changed his behavior to the extent that they were willing to give him another chance. Farrell targeted a race at Golden Gate Fields in northern California on April 19, 1965.

The day of the race turned out to be stormy and Hey Sam would have to run in a downpour. All the elements seemed to be against us, but Hey Sam performed like a true champion and won. He ran the six furlongs in 1:11.03, winning by ten lengths and earning the right to be called a "superior mudder" for the balance of his career. A photograph of the winner included Joe Perreira in a black topcoat. Joe was Sam's regular exercise rider, and I remember him saying that riding him was like riding Citation against the field.

Hey Sam went on to win fourteen races and earn over $100,000. He and I had had our challenges, but it seems we both met them and learned from the experience. I felt such pride in his success, as a parent would seeing his wayward child get straight A's on his report card. Hey Sam became—as I had hoped he would—my entrée into the world of Thoroughbred racing, an industry that would prove to be the focus of my career for the next forty years.

BARLET

I had just arrived on the show grounds of the Cow Palace in San Francisco for the 1962 Quarter Horse National Championships when Marten Clark made me an offer. His horse, Barlet, was favored to win Grand Champion Stallion—most thought it a virtual certainty—but Clark had not been able to get the horse out of his box stall for two days.

I had first met Barlet while working as a stunt rider on a Disney film called *The Horse with the Flying Tail*, which was shot on location in the Salinas Valley. Barlet was just a foal then, playing the early years of the equine star, a palomino jumping horse. The actor Slim Pickens, whom I'd known since I was a child, was also in the film. I remember him playing tricks with little Barlet, who was just like a puppy. Slim would throw a stick and Barlet would bring it back to him. When Slim slapped his chest, calling "Hup, hup!" the foal would jump up and put his front legs on Slim's shoulders. It seemed cute at the time, but later, when Barlet was a 1,000-pound two-year-old, it definitely wasn't. Barlet continued to try to jump on people, striking out dangerously with his front legs. Another favorite pastime of his was to bite, causing serious injury to his victims.

Before Barlet was ridden, Clark began showing him throughout the western United States. He became a champion halter horse in a competition that judges conformation, or anatomical excellence, to determine which horse is the closest to the model for the breed. But Barlet was difficult as a result of his early experiences. He was overhumanized and had become troubled and mean as a result.

By the time I saw him again at the National Championships, he was being kept in a stall surrounded with electrified wires. Without them, Barlet would slash at the walls with his teeth and kick them with his hind legs whenever another horse or person passed by. Marten told me that if I could get Barlet out of the stall to the show ring and win, he'd give me a half interest in him. Then I could take him back to San Luis Obispo and put him in training to ride and show.

As a national champion, Barlet would have a value somewhere in the range of $35,000. I knew he'd be a challenge, but I was convinced there wasn't a horse that I couldn't handle. I opened the door of the box stall. There was Barlet with his teeth bared and his ears pinned back, charging at me. I quickly slammed the door shut and stepped back to reassess the situation.

Don Dodge, a former instructor of mine, had once shown me a device he called a "come-along," which was a long rope wound and knotted around the horse's head in a halterlike fashion. It provided far more control than a traditional halter. It would shrink and become uncomfortable if the horse resisted it, and expand and become relaxed when he cooperated with it. I went to my equipment bag and got the necessary rope. With a bit of luck, a lot of experience and a young body, I was able to get the come-along on Barlet without being injured. With the rope in place, I felt relatively confident that I could control him.

Marten opened the door and I led Barlet out of the stall and into a training lane where the footing was good. I walked him forward several times, stopping short and then correcting him with the rope if he barged into my space. I schooled him to back up, and though he was very resistant at first, I could soon see a significant improvement in his level of respect.

I decided to fashion a show halter for the competition the following day that would approximate the effect of the come-along. It worked. I showed Barlet and he won his national championship. Pat and I became half owners of the handsome horse and he started training with us. Later he was successful in the hackamore division with me on his back.

Though my join-up method went some way to helping Barlet, there was never a day when I could completely trust him. He never forgot how to be mean, and we had to be very careful around him, never allowing an inexperienced person to handle him. I've since met a number of mean horses, but he was definitely the meanest I had met to that time and so looms quite large in the scheme of my education. He demanded exceptional horsemanship from me, and I found his lessons extremely valuable in later years as I encountered many more horses with vicious tendencies. Without him in my life, I wouldn't be as capable with horses today.

Barlet winning his national Championship for the Open Quarter Horse Stallions in 1963. I'm at his head with Charles Araujo presenting.

FIDDLE D'OR

Fiddle D'Or was an attractive palomino foal, considered well-bred for a Quarter Horse of his day. He was foaled in 1956 in Tulare, California, bred by Perry Cotton, who owned the dam and also had an interest in the sire, Bras D'Or. A couple of years before Fiddle D'Or was born, I met Homer Mitchell, who had purchased a nearby San Luis Obispo property on which to retire. He wanted me to train some horses for him and felt that Fiddle had potential. He purchased him as a weanling.

Fiddle was brought to me at two years of age, and he showed a great deal of ability as he ran with the other horses. He had slightly straight hind legs, but his coordination was exemplary and he could run, stop and turn with the grace of a ballet dancer. He also seemed to be a steady individual without keen sensitivity or nervous tendencies. He had what you might call "quiet confidence."

I started him using join-up in the round pen and liked him immediately. Though he wasn't the brightest of horses, he made that count to his advantage—he didn't fuss or worry too much. The task was there, you did it—that was his attitude. He was like a journeyman athlete and he was a pleasure to work with. I began the process of schooling him to turn, stop and do figure eights. I worked him on cattle because I felt he would be best suited to the reined cow horse division. Fiddle's cow work and his spins were his strongest points from very early on in his career.

With his slightly straight hind legs, sliding stops were not so easy for

Fiddle, but he would try for you every working day. His flying lead changes were a testament to true athleticism and he remains one of the outstanding working cow horses where figure eights are concerned.

For years I had been thinking about training horses to turn in a different way than they were used to. I was convinced that performance horses could turn more efficiently if they crouched closer to the ground rather than elevating their body. My new student proved my theory was correct, and he became one of the very first Western horses to spin by locking his hind legs in place and pivoting around one hind foot, almost literally drilling a hole in the ground. He was a forerunner of the successful reining and working cow horses today.

I began to show Fiddle as a four-year-old in 1960. We started at Clements, California, in May and went on from there, never finishing lower than third and coming first about 80 percent of the time. During his first season of competition we won at many of the nation's largest shows, including a victory on the grounds where I was born and raised in Salinas. By the first week in November he was the World Champion Hackamore Horse with the National Reined Cow Horse Association. Being second two years in a row with My Blue Heaven had only added to my hunger for a world championship with a reined cow horse. While I had won a world championship in the junior division and two national championships in rodeo, this was my first world championship in open professional competition with a reined cow horse. I was extra proud of this accomplishment because it seemed to establish me in the world of professional horse training.

I decided to keep Fiddle D'Or in the hackamore—that is, headgear without a metal bit—for his fifth year. This was an unusual step because most horses are hard to keep responsive and light in the hackamore under heavy showing for prolonged periods. I was competing in about forty shows a season, and it would be unprecedented if I could maintain Fiddle's record through 1961. I thought Fiddle might just do it because he loved his cattle work so much.

During the months I prepared Fiddle for his second year of competition, I remembered so clearly the lessons Brownie had taught me about easing up on his schedule and allowing him to have fun. Fiddle didn't need to

Fiddle D'Or in winning form: here he is at the trophy presentation for one of his world championship victories—World Champion Hackamore Horse, 1960 and 1961.

practice our stops and spins. Working cattle was a joy for him and, if I kept him physically fit, working a cow three or four times a week was all he needed to give me winning performances on the weekends.

I suppose Fiddle, more than any other horse, taught me that work should be the only discipline and that relaxation was the best reward. If he made a mistake on a cow, I would put pressure on him, asking him to recover control of the animal as quickly as he could. On the other hand, when he was in full control and making difficult moves look easy, I would stop him, get off, stroke his head and let his adrenaline subside. He came to love this routine and I think it's the reason he won his second world championship in 1961.

Fiddle was an awesome horse and he simply ruled the hackamore division of the National Reined Cow Horse Association for his final season. His win ratio was close to 90 percent and he was never below third place. So far as I know, Fiddle is still the only horse in history ever to win the hackamore championship two years running. With the fierce competition of the modern day, it's not likely we'll see his record broken.

SCOTTY

Harley May, originally of Deming, New Mexico, was one of the greatest all-around performers in the history of rodeo. Harley could rope as well as ride bucking horses or bulls, and while he worked every event that rodeo has to offer, bulldogging was his favorite as well as his most successful.

Harley told me that one of the prizes he was given for winning the All-Around Championship in a South Dakota rodeo some years previously was a dark chestnut colt. A friend had raised the horse for him but he needed a lot of training. As it turned out, that friend was Bob Scott, which is why he named the foal Scotty. I had gone to school with Bob and shown horses with him as well. Harley wanted me to train Scotty to compete in bulldogging.

Scotty arrived in late 1961. Although he was green, he would accept the saddle and rider, so it was time for more advanced training. I always kept a few steers around the place because I loved to practice bulldogging, and I made time each day to work on Scotty's skills. The early exercises were designed to train him to understand that he needed to run past the left side of the animal, allowing me to slide off his back and onto the steer's withers. As soon as my weight was on the steer, Scotty had to move forward rapidly and slightly to the left, so that my feet could make contact with the ground without his interference. Within a month or two, Scotty was allowing me to catch cattle. He was quick to learn and I enjoyed teaching him the elements of reining and working a cow. I tried to give him a good foundation so that he would enjoy his work and be cooperative, and he was fun to work with. Within six months or so I was recommending that John W. Jones try him out.

John W. was my traveling partner in rodeo back then, and I would usually ride whatever horse he had at the time. While I had Scotty, John W. was riding a horse called Blue. I didn't like Blue as a rodeo horse; he would let you down just when you needed him the most. Blue didn't have the fire in his belly that Scotty had, and often just as you were catching a steer, he would cut across so that your feet hit the ground in front of the steer, causing it to somersault over top of you. This is not a wonderful experience and can, in fact, produce serious injury. I've seen several cowboys suffer broken limbs and head injuries because of somersaults. During my career as a bulldogger I took several somersaults but fortunately escaped getting seriously hurt.

One time John W. and I traveled about fifteen miles to a neighbor's ranch to practice bulldogging. The guy had some steers that were going to waste, and John and I had agreed to give them some exercise. He had a wonderful arena and everything was perfect. Pat came along to help with our practice.

When we arrived, we found a note pinned to the front door saying that our friend had had to go away for a meeting, but the steers were there and we should make ourselves at home. We drove down to the arena, which was about three hundred yards from the house, loaded the steers into the chute, warmed up our horses and got ready to go. As I recall, we had two horses with us: Blue to bulldog from and Dude to haze with. Dude's job was to keep the steer running straight so the bulldogger could catch hold of the horns without the steer ducking away.

John W. ran the first steer and did a good job with it. After letting the horses catch their breath for a few minutes, I backed Blue into the starting box and prepared to make my run. Pat, sitting on a seat on top of the chute, was in charge of opening the gate. She had to step on a pedal to release the latch and allow the steer to run into the arena.

I nodded my head to Pat, and Blue stormed out of the box. He got me to the steer in good shape but just as I was catching hold of the horns, he

OVERLEAF *Scotty's first run for me, in the Grand National Rodeo, Grand National Cow Palace, San Francisco, 1962. Champion Harley May is the hazer. Scotty got me to this first steer like the champion he later became.*

made a right turn into the animal's path. My feet came down across the steer's center axis, almost under Dude's feet on the far side. The effect was like thrusting a stick between the steer's front legs, except it was no stick— it was my legs. Down we went.

The steer pushed its face right into the sand and then did a somersault over top of me. Now his head was on my left and his body was twisted around my right side with his tail touching the ground over to my left, where his head was. I was in a steer sandwich. I could hardly breathe and the steer couldn't seem to move at all.

Any well-meaning partner would jump off his horse, grab the steer's tail and pull, allowing the steer to regain its feet and releasing the bulldogger from the tangle. John W. was anything but a well-meaning partner! He leisurely rode Dude back toward me as I yelled at him to get the steer off me.

"Pat," he called. "What do you want from him? What do you need? We got him where we want him now!"

I am not sure exactly what I said for the next twenty seconds or so, but the language I used wouldn't be fit for publication.

John W. eventually hauled the steer off me. Luckily, I was not injured and the steer was perfectly fine. What wasn't fine was my memory of how Blue had cut me off. I told John W. that I had a young horse coming on that would be much better than Blue, and that he had to seriously consider making Scotty our primary bulldogging horse.

But the best I could do over the next few months was convince John W. to buy Scotty from Harley May. I was pleased that we now owned Scotty, but unhappy that I couldn't convince John to take him to rodeos instead of Blue. The only reason John had bought Scotty was that his wife, JoAnn, wanted him as a barrel racing horse. As far as I was concerned, we had the wrong horse on the bulldogging team.

All through 1962 and '63 John W. resisted my efforts to make the change. We had a race one day and Blue actually outran Scotty, which surprised me no end and further convinced John that Blue was the right horse for the job. Bulldogging is a timed event and acceleration is of critical importance.

I believe it was in November 1962 at the Cow Palace that I drew a good steer in the first round and Blue cut me off again. I was furious. The fact that Scotty was 250 miles away and I was riding Blue made no sense, so I drove through the night to fetch Scotty for his first run in actual competition.

The Cow Palace was not the place you would normally start a green horse. It was the premier arena for Western competition and rodeo. But Scotty allowed me to catch a steer in perfect shape, which should have proved to John W. that he was the horse to use.

It didn't. Scotty couldn't get on the right side of John W., and late in 1963 he sold the horse to Walter Wyatt of Bakersfield, California. Walter kept him for a few months before selling him to Walt Linderman of Red Lodge, Montana. Walt was a nephew of the great Bill Linderman, a multiple world champion bulldogger, and was interested in putting together a bulldogging team. The usual arrangement was that if a bulldogger didn't own his horse, he paid one-eighth of his winnings to the owner, with another eighth going to the hazer. Putting together a bulldogging team usually meant that one person owned both horses and so received a quarter of the earnings.

Walt hit the road in late 1964 with a good haze horse and Scotty. The record this horse created in the next twelve years was absolutely unbelievable. Scotty was responsible for two cowboys winning three world championships. Ironically enough, one of them was Harley May, who became the world champion bulldogger in 1965. The other was Jack Roddy, who won on Scotty in 1966 and 1968. Walt won three runner-up titles, in 1966, '70 and '71.

The National Finals Rodeo accepts only the top fifteen bulldoggers each year and Scotty won five times, four consecutively, which was unheard of. Guess who won on him in 1965 and '68: John W. Jones!

When Scotty reached fourteen years of age, in 1971, he retired from professional competition and became the favorite bulldogging horse of many high school and college cowboys. Scotty enjoyed his work so much that I figure, if he'd had his way, he'd have been out there running past steers all on his own. Horses are excited by competition, and in the absence of force, they'll love it as much as people do.

At twenty years of age, Scotty went to live with the Yedder family, who agreed to keep him at pasture for the rest of his life. He'd never been sick or lame, and he died of natural causes about five years later. If you've ever owned a horse, you'll know why I included Scotty in this book. I competed on him a limited number of times and personally won no championships on him, but his earnings for his riders ran into millions of dollars. His honesty and dedication to his craft were overwhelming. I am proud to have played a small part in giving Scotty his early training. He became the champion he deserved to be.

NIGHT MIST

Night Mist was with me at the same time Scotty was, and they traveled together countless times. I can still picture them side by side in that trailer decades ago and here they are again, side by side in this book.

Perry Cotton of Tulare, California, raised many good Quarter Horses during the 1940s, '50s and '60s, one of which was Midnight III, a blue roan stallion of Hancock breeding. When bred to Lucky Lady Tucker by Lucky Blanton, Midnight III produced a blue roan filly, later to be named Night Mist.

W. D. Dana had a horse operation at Healdsburg, located in the heart of northern California's wine country. Originally a New York businessman—at one time he owned the Empire State Building—Mr. Dana became interested in the tradition of the reined cow horses of the west. He bought a property and hired one of the best Western trainers I have ever known, John Brazil. It was on John's recommendation that Mr. Dana bought Night Mist as a yearling. John started Night Mist in late 1960 and showed her very lightly in 1962 with significant success.

In 1963 Mr. Dana passed away, and the following year his horse holdings in northern California were auctioned. I was showing and unable to attend, so Pat represented us. We had already asked our friends John and Glory Bacon whether they would be interested in purchasing Night Mist with us. John Bacon and I had been friends since we went to Cal Poly together, and now that we were both married, we often took vacations

together with our wives. Once, on a trip to Mexico, John and I raced our horses back to our hotel. We had laid bets on who would get to the bar first and, rather than dismount, we rode our horses right into the hotel, across the foyer and up the stairs to the bar on the second floor. We called it a dead heat, and on the way back out, John took a moment to build a loop and make a perfect throw over the head of a mannequin standing in front of the dress shop. He dragged the dummy off the pedestal, across the lobby and out of the hotel's main entrance, causing an incoming guest to nearly faint with surprise. She thought a real person was being dragged off.

John Bacon came from a very wealthy industrial family and could ride well but had never been involved in competition. We had been partners in a few minor horses and had bred some mares together, but Night Mist was going to cost serious money. John could afford to put up a significant sum, and I was prepared to maintain and train the mare as my side of the partnership. This would be our first venture into the area of high-level show horses. If I did my work well, I believed I had a chance of producing a world champion.

The Bacons agreed to the proposal, Pat was successful at the auction, and Night Mist arrived at our farm. John Brazil had done a good job of building a foundation for her. She was a willing worker and I suppose it's fair to say that the greatest challenge we faced was getting to know each other. She seemed to have talent as a reined cow horse, but like all horses she had her idiosyncrasies that I would have to become accustomed to. After a few months of basic get-acquainted work, I felt we were ready for open competition. Night Mist was a wonderful mare to work with. She'd give you 100 percent if you presented the challenges properly. And she seemed to gravitate toward children. Curiously enough, the Bacons had two girls and a boy, just as we did, and the children all took to calling her "Nice Mist." The nickname stuck for the rest of her life.

Night Mist came along at a time when I wanted to concentrate on working with our Quarter Horse stallion, Johnny Tivio, whose story comes last in this book. I had been showing Johnny Tivio in both the cutting and

Night Mist: World Champion Working Cow Horse, 1964 and 1965. Shown here at home on Flag Is Up after retirement.

working cow horse classes before Night Mist arrived. She gave me the opportunity to enter Johnny Tivio in the cutting horse division only. And she filled the bill for the working cow horse classes in a way no one could have dreamed possible. She was faster, stopped harder and turned more quickly than any of the experts had predicted she would.

An interesting situation arose in our first competition together. You have to ride an open reined cow horse with the reins in one hand and with no fingers between the reins. Somehow Night Mist had developed a tendency to move slightly to the left as she galloped the straight lines that are part of every reined cow horse pattern. This tendency had not been apparent in practice but, with the tension of competition, it was definitely there.

I had always ridden my horses using my left hand—as most competitors do—but after that competition I reversed the process and began riding Night Mist holding the reins with my right hand. It was awkward at first but it didn't take long to see that Night Mist preferred it. In our second competition together she performed much better. To this day I don't know why she needed that change of hands; all I know is that it worked.

I showed Night Mist throughout the seasons of 1964 and '65 with high hopes. She accepted every lesson and always maintained her world-class competitive edge, becoming world champion in both seasons. I remember the day Pat told me we had just passed the thirty victories point in less than two years. Night Mist was never below third place.

I won the Grand National at the Cow Palace on Night Mist. As a team we won a saddle at Salinas and again in Santa Barbara in the same year. In 1965 we made a successful swing through Arizona, New Mexico and Texas with wins in Phoenix, Albuquerque, Fort Worth, El Paso and Houston. The Western horsemen of New Mexico and Texas knew practically nothing about California reining horses, and they marveled at her ability.

In 1966, as I completed my cow work for the championship class, I felt Night Mist stumble and almost fall. We happened to be right at the end of our work and our score wasn't affected. When I came back in for the trophy presentation, I noticed her pointing her left foreleg a little as we stood in line. Naturally I was worried and I bandaged her knee with a poultice that night. When I returned to her stall in the morning, she was definitely lame at the walk. I got her home as quickly as I could.

Radiographs indicated she had a slight fracture in one of the carpal bones in the near, or left, knee.

We and the Bacons decided it was time to retire Night Mist. She had given so much to the people in her life and it was time to allow her a pasture, green grass and motherhood. We bred her to Johnny Tivio early in 1967 and the result was a chestnut colt with some roan in his flanks. Pat named him Mr. Tiv. He went on to win two world championships with the National Reined Cow Horse Association under a rider by the name of Jody Gearhart.

Night Mist had known how to rise to an important occasion and she was a wonderful equine partner to travel with, with her sweet and friendly disposition. Her last days were spent among her loving family of mares until she died one night in her field and was buried in our horse graveyard. Her memorial stone reads, "Night Mist 1958–1986. World Champion Reined Cow Horse. Winner of 31 consecutive classes. Owned by John Bacon and Monty Roberts." Those are the bare facts. The emotions are impossible to describe.

SERGEANT

Memories that were dormant for decades have been aroused during the writing of this book. Some take me back to deeply emotional times, to situations that brought joy or sadness, but when I remember Sergeant, I just have to smile.

It was 1966 and I was planning to show Night Mist at Monterey, California, which would turn out to be her last time. Pat was encouraging me to enter the open roping at the same competition and, in fact, had entered us in the mixed team roping as well.

"I don't have a horse!" I objected. Bernie was long gone and I hadn't owned a decent horse for roping heels for several years. Pat said she'd already taken care of that. One of her cousins, Bill Lambert, had agreed to provide us with horses to rope on. I asked what horse I was going ride and she replied, "Old Sergeant."

Sergeant had been a darn good heel horse in his day and was now about seventeen or eighteen years old. I had roped on him dozens of times and liked him. He was a good choice.

Jerry Matney brought Sergeant and another horse from the Lambert Ranch to the Monterey County Fairgrounds, about thirty miles away. Both horses had been used on the ranch; although Pat's mount had shoes that were adequate, Sergeant's feet looked terrible. I asked Pat to make arrangements with the on-duty farrier to get some new shoes on him before the competition began the following day.

The farrier was Bill Whitney, an old friend who'd been our farrier at the Salinas Rodeo Competition Grounds for most of the postwar years. He was quite old by this time, and when he saw the burrs in Sergeant's mane and tail and his overall raunchy look, suggesting he might be a bit wild, Bill asked me if the horse was gentle. I reassured him that there was no question that Sergeant was gentle—that was a given.

Bill suggested I return in about an hour and a half. Pat and I called in at the horse show and rodeo office to go through the necessary check-in routine, had a hamburger and then moseyed back to collect Sergeant. As we walked up, we both realized that something was wrong. Bill's assistant was walking briskly toward us and he had a disconcerting look about him. His eyes were open just a little too wide and his shoulders seemed a bit stiff.

"Bill's gone to the doctor," he said. "Sergeant kicked him and they took him away in an ambulance."

"What?" I said. "That's not possible. Sergeant's never kicked anybody in his life!"

The assistant told us that Sergeant had stood calmly while three shoes were easily fixed in place. In fact, he was so placid it seemed as though he'd fallen into a deep sleep. Then, when his leg was picked up for the last shoe, he suddenly exploded, blew hard through his nose, kicked out, pulled back and tried to run away all at the same time, catching Bill on the leg. His behavior was incomprehensible.

The assistant agreed to put on Sergeant's last shoe and while he was doing it, Bill appeared. He had a slight limp and showed us the bandage under his jeans. We asked what he thought had gone wrong. Fortunately, Bill smiled.

"Monty, I disturbed that horse while he was dreaming about a lion," he said. "There's no doubt in my mind about it."

Sergeant didn't make a move while the last shoe was nailed on, Pat and I were able to rope, and Bill Whitney was OK to continue his shoeing for the balance of the show.

I've had many dreams about horses—Pat has often been woken by an arm landing across her face as I've dreamed of being bucked off. As a child, I dreamed of riding into the mountains, hiding away, escaping. Then I would watch myself getting stuck in the wrong place—dreams of panic and pursuit. When I was dealing with Barlet, I dreamed of being devoured by a horse. But do horses dream? Who knows? It's a question that has been bandied about for generations, and I suppose the debate will continue until someone straps a machine on a horse that proves it one way or another. For me, I'd just like to continue thinking they do.

JULIA'S DOLL

Pat was never a competition rider as a youngster but she loved horses nonetheless. She rode in Salinas when she was growing up, and her grandfather had a horse called Poncho, who provided her with lasting memories.

By 1962 we'd been married for six years. We had three children and the eldest, Debbie, was riding. Pat was ready to get back in the saddle and maybe start competing. Then along came Julia's Doll.

It was November when Dr. Stephen Jensen of Paicines, California, sent four Quarter Horse fillies to our San Luis Obispo training operation. He had a price on each of them and asked that we get them started under saddle and promote their sale. Three of the fillies were decent, and he had priced them at around $1,500 each. They were well-bred and easy to start, and I think we found homes for them in a short period of time.

The fourth filly was an absolute gem. Julia's Doll was by Poco Rey out of Spanishsprings Julia. She was nineteen months of age and as pretty a filly as Mother Nature could create. Julia's Doll had the muscling of a world-class Quarter Horse but the elegance and femininity of an Egyptian Arab. She was trim and petite where appropriate, and strong and rugged where a Quarter Horse was meant to be.

She was one classy lady, and it seemed to me that she was meant to be shown by a female. I told Pat that she'd better start honing her skills, because we had a potential champion in our midst and she was crying out for a woman to show her.

Dr. Jensen had put a price of $2,500 on Julia's Doll. I thought she was worth closer to $6,000 to $7,000. Today, Julia would command a price somewhere close to $100,000.

Pat tells me that she remembers seeing me ride Julia that first day in the arena, and that she was producing flying lead changes before knowing the rider's signals. She was so coordinated that it was simple for her to make changes without becoming disunited. This is a rare quality found in very few young horses.

However, Julia's Doll was not a reined cow horse. Running, sliding and working a dirty old cow were not what she was cut out to do. She was the

Julia's Doll shown winning one of her many championships with
Pat in the saddle in 1966

epitome of a Western pleasure horse. She moved with the cheetah's silken quality. Her temperament was one of complete cooperation. Congeniality was a byword for this filly.

Julia's Doll was shown in hand in the spring of 1963. Pat also entered her in a few Western pleasure classes under saddle. To experienced horsemen this may seem an outrageous claim, but the record shows that in May, with only about six months of riding, Pat rode two-year-old Julia's Doll in an open Western pleasure class in Danville, California, and won. It was a sign of things to come.

For the next three years, Pat and Julia's Doll ruled the female halter division and reigned supreme over the Western pleasure classes of the western part of the United States. Julia's Doll earned a Register of Merit in Performance and Superior Halter as well as achieving the status of American Quarter Horse Association Champion in 1964. Her trophies for grand championships line a long shelf in my office to this day. Not only was she a joy for Pat to train and show, but Julia's Doll found joy in it, too. Together they created an elegant picture in the show ring. Julia was beautiful to look at and she possessed the sweetest of dispositions, too. Those two characteristics made her Pat's dream horse and she feels lucky to have had her in her life.

After retirement from the show ring, Julia's Doll raised fourteen foals, producing some of the most important Quarter Horses of our time. She and her daughters produced literally hundreds of thousands of dollars' worth of young Quarter Horse prospects and affected the Quarter Horse industry in countries beyond the United States, including Canada, Israel and Brazil.

Julia's Doll died in 1988 and is buried in our horse graveyard. Her headstone reads: "Julia gave 27 years of pleasure and left an outstanding legacy through her produce."

The strongest lesson Julia's Doll taught me is that a good trainer needs to bury his ego and respect the wishes of his equine students. Find the thing they want to do most and help them do it, even if it doesn't involve you personally. A selfish attitude in training horses will eventually come back to haunt you, as it will in human relationships. Julia might have done well in open competition under me, but I can't conceive of her doing nearly as well as she did with Pat.

BAHROONA

My dream of training Thoroughbred racehorses dominated every night's sleep throughout the early sixties. I had loved every minute of my experience with Hey Sam and felt I could contribute a great deal to racing. In my mind, Thoroughbred racehorses seemed to be calling out to me, and I was compelled to answer the challenge. I felt in my bones that the next stone in my necklace would be a racehorse; I just had to find him or her.

I had purchased a few Thoroughbreds for California owners during the early sixties, but limited funds had sent me to sales of lower-quality animals. I recall one owner sending me to a third-rate sale in Pomona, California, with the agreement that I could buy as many yearlings as I liked, so long as their conformation was near perfect and I stayed under $2,000.

Of course, there is no such thing as a cheap horse. Each and every one is of equal value in the most important ways and certainly should be treated as such. I was determined to avoid the trap fallen into by some racehorse trainers who placed bets on their own horses and deliberately altered their training to improve their financial bottom line. I made a promise to myself that I would never bet on horses, and I've stuck to it.

In 1964 I was approached by Hastings Harcourt of Santa Barbara, California. He was the son of the founder of the Harcourt Brace publishing company and was an unfortunate-looking man. He had a bad skin condition; his face was pitted and marked. He wore thick spectacles, he was bulky—tall but overweight and soft—and he was enormously wealthy. His was old-world money. Families such as his had owned racehorses since the long-distant past. He was well connected to other leading families, with blueblood friends who met at the Turf Club and at the races. Mr. Harcourt and his wife wanted not only to join in this world of high-level racing but to triumph in it with horses they owned.

I had trained a Western pleasure horse, Travel's Echo, for Mr. Harcourt that was very successful during the 1964 show season. As a consequence, he suggested sending me to the 1965 Del Mar Thoroughbred yearling sale so that I might select a few prospects with the intention of racing them on southern California's premier tracks. He proposed a budget of $50,000 to buy three or four yearlings. Was I interested?

Can you imagine how I felt hearing I would have a budget of $50,000 after being limited to around $2,000 per horse in the past? It took a fraction of a second for me to answer that question. Yes, I was more than interested.

I went home and studied every book and magazine I could get my hands on. I tracked the results of horses I had liked from previous sales. I spent countless hours preparing myself to make an intelligent decision when the time came to raise my hand and spend Mr. Harcourt's money.

Del Mar is a racetrack near San Diego. Ever since Bing Crosby founded it in the 1930s, it has remained the site of the premier Thoroughbred yearling sale for California breeders. In the mid-sixties the average yearling price, as I recall, was around $20,000 to $30,000. Many of the horses running in California races came from the big sales in Kentucky, Florida and New York, with average prices significantly higher than Del Mar's. We were still paying fairly little money, but I was convinced I could find a winner.

Pat and I went to Del Mar in September 1965. I carried a sales catalog filled with notes of the research I had done and had a pulse rate that would have scared any doctor. We walked the grounds at first to get acquainted with the sales procedures and locate the various consignors of horses that had attracted our interest. Pat read out the records of sires and information about the quality of races won by sisters and brothers of the horses for sale. To say that I was well prepared would have been an understatement, but as soon as I began to examine the yearlings I settled down. I realized that my most important asset was not so much my recently acquired knowledge of the catalog—anyone could look up a pedigree—but my instinctive understanding of horses. That was my particular skill. Pat agreed; we were getting too technical with all of the research. There wasn't one yearling there that could read a pedigree.

While standing on a particular spot that will be forever burned into my memory, I noticed a blood bay colt walk from right to left across my line of sight. He was about twenty yards from me and was being led from one barn to another. He immediately caught my attention and we followed him, turning at the end of the stable and walking about another twenty yards. As we approached the consignment that included this yearling, we stopped and stood back as he was taken to his assigned stall. The handler removed the lead shank and closed a screen in front of him. It was the type of gate that allowed the horse to put his head out, and I watched his reaction to the activity outside.

I was captivated by what I considered to be a very bright but calm individual who seemed in full control of the nervous energy that appeared to be present in his frame in vast quantities. The card on the outside of his stall informed us he was hip number 65 and by Poona II out of In Regards by With Regards. We asked to see him.

No fewer than three attendants began to scurry around with lead shanks, brushes, hoof picks and even a can of hoof dressing. Good God, where I had been buying horses up until then, you'd be lucky if they even found a halter to lead them out. I've never asked Pat, but I suppose she felt strange as well, as we stood there like a couple of wealthy prospective buyers. It was an uncomfortable feeling and one that I must admit has not left me to this day.

The yearling was led out for us and I was blown away by the quality of his conformation. The triangle (which is shown on page 92) was so good it overwhelmed me. The shoulder and the hip complemented each other in a way that made his movement catlike. Few horses I had ever seen were as coordinated. My pulse shot up, and I realized I was in danger of giving away how interested I was in him.

I decided to spend a lot of time around that stable as the day went on, standing back and watching others view this yearling, assessing him to see how he fared with the tiring hours of inspection. His character stayed pure, unlike so many yearlings who grow angry at having to make repeated trips in and out of the stable. He continued to impress me until the moment he entered the sales ring.

As I recall, the bidding started off at around the $2,000 to $3,000 level. I had spent a lot of time at horse and cattle auctions, but although I counted myself an experienced bidder, I just wasn't accustomed to spending large sums of money for one horse. I stayed out of the bidding until it slowed down at around $5,000. I whispered to Pat that I was willing to go to about $15,000 for what I perceived to be the best individual in the sale. I think my first bid was $5,500. Soon I was trading bids with one other buyer, but I registered the winning bid at $6,500.

I was worried by the low price. Was there something I didn't know? It didn't seem possible that others wouldn't pay more for him. Prior to hip number 65, several physically inferior horses had sold in the $30,000 to $40,000 range.

I took the colt home and met Mr. Harcourt within a day or so to show him off. His reaction was a bit negative. He said that he'd sent me to the sale to buy horses of high quality with a good chance of winning races at the major tracks of southern California. He'd expected to pay $15,000 to $20,000 for each yearling. He believed that the price was likely to indicate how the horse would perform on the racecourse. I knew that genetics played a large role in the success or failure of racehorses and I asked him to trust me.

Without explaining join-up to Mr. Harcourt, I said that I would like the chance to train the young horse using my particular methods. I felt I could turn him into a willing partner in racing and get him to use the best of his ability. Mr. Harcourt really had no choice in the matter, and although he was reluctant he was still hopeful—after all, I had succeeded with his show horse the previous year in dramatic fashion. Mrs. Harcourt asked if the colt had a name, and I explained that choosing a name was the privilege of the owner. Mr. Harcourt suggested that his wife should select a name.

We discussed the colt's breeding. His sire, Poona II, was an Irish import with exceptional ability as a sprinter. California was the stronghold of world-quality sprinters, and many of our races were organized with this in mind. I explained that In Regards was a mare that possessed blinding speed but was unable to hold that speed for the classic distances. She was the winner of an internationally approved stakes race.

There are Formula One horses and then there are drag racers, and I explained that I expected this colt to be a drag racer. With that Mrs. Harcourt said she had the perfect name for him.

"*Bahrooona!* Doesn't that sound like a dragster?" Mrs. Harcourt asked. We agreed it did and he was registered as Bahroona, a name that stayed with him throughout his life.

Bahroona was a terrific student and went through seven or eight months of preparatory work without a negative moment. Whether it was the result of my training technique or his inherited personality, he was obliging and kind and proved to be every bit the athlete I'd hoped he'd be. He was all boy, strong, muscular and full of energy. I sent him off to the trainer Farrell Jones with great expectations. In the world of Thoroughbred racing, there are licensed trainers who remain at the racetracks and train the racehorses there. I've never wanted to become a racetrack trainer. My lot in life has been to prepare them for and manage their careers.

Farrell and I were having breakfast with a group of trainers in the track kitchen at Hollywood Park one morning in early June when we agreed to target Bahroona for a race in July. It would prepare him for a major internationally approved stakes race due to be run back at Del Mar on September 10, almost exactly one year from the date of Bahroona's purchase. I remember one of the other trainers saying, "He's got to break his maiden [win his first race] before you start thinking about stakes races." Farrell spoke up immediately.

"I think I've got a weapon here, at least for the sprints," he said.

If Bahroona didn't perform well enough to win his maiden race, there would still be time to give him a second race before the stake. Bahroona's workouts were good, but Farrell was not the type of trainer to put undue pressure on young horses, so we couldn't know his maximum speed potential yet.

I got a call from Farrell around July 15 to say that Bahroona was entered for his maiden race on a Sunday, about ten days later. I told Farrell I was bulldogging and showing cutting and reined cow horses that day in San Juan Bautista.

"I don't care what you're doing," he said. "This race is right for him and he's ready for it."

I called Mr. Harcourt and told him I would have to see Bahroona's first race on video the following week because of my commitment.

"Not on your life," he said. "I'll send my plane to San Juan and fly you straight to Hollywood Park."

I thought I'd be finished with my competition by about one o'clock, and the race wasn't scheduled to go off until about five thirty. Mr. Harcourt said he'd send a King Air to get me there in time.

I arrived at the Hawthorne airport with a car and driver waiting and made it to the track in time to go to the saddling paddock about half an hour before the race. I sat up in the Harcourt box watching while they loaded the horses in the starting gate. The gates opened and twelve horses bolted out, each one straining to be in front.

They went into the first turn with Bahroona about two lengths in front of the field. He opened up ten lengths in the final hundred yards and won by the widest margin ever posted at Hollywood Park for a maiden victory. We were all overwhelmed with excitement. We dashed to the winner's circle and basked in the glorious triumph. I still have the photograph of us crowding around Bahroona, elated and surprised, our arms around one another's shoulders.

Bahroona rested through the month of August and then went on to win the Graduation Stakes at Del Mar by a margin of five lengths. He won $80,000 in two races, all within twelve months of that moment I first saw him walk by.

The success of Bahroona accelerated Mr. Harcourt's interest in setting up a world-class Thoroughbred racehorse establishment. He had already sent me to Europe on a nonstop month-long tour to look at all the major racing establishments in England, Ireland, France and Germany. A private plane had been put at our disposal to cover the ground more quickly. I came back with a plan in my head of exactly what I wanted and where it should be located. Mr. Harcourt agreed with my ideas and bought twelve hundred acres of real estate in the Santa Ynez Valley near Solvang, California. Within eighteen months he'd spent $3.6 million in creating Flag Is Up Farms, complete with a breeding and foaling facility, a training and starting center with stalls for eighty horses, a training track, two and a half miles of cross-country gallops and a fully equipped hospital and rehabilitation center.

On a hill overlooking the farm, a ranch house was built for Pat and me and our young family. It was designed in the early Californian style with extensive south-facing views over the valley.

I also had a round pen built that was completely enclosed in heavy tongue-and-groove boards. No one could see in. Once I swung the heavy door shut behind me, no one would know what I was doing. I had become accustomed to keeping my secret. At some stage it would be right to show someone my concepts but not now. On the strength of one winner, I had been given the biggest break ever handed to a young trainer of horses, and I couldn't jeopardize it.

The triangle, as drawn for me by the staff of the University of Zurich

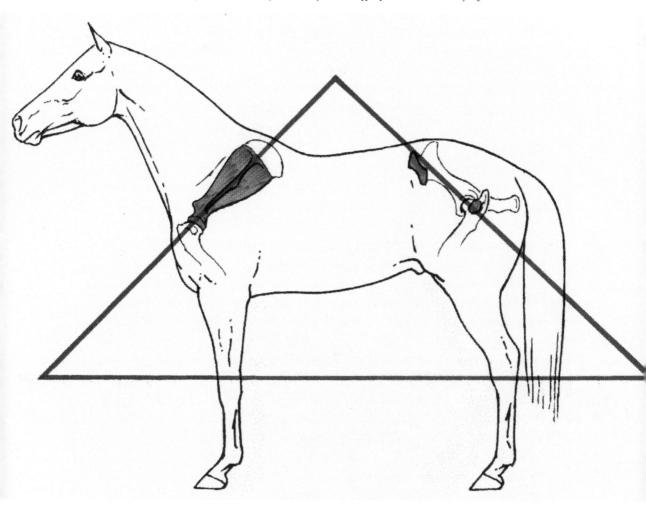

SHARIVARI

While Bahroona was winning the Graduation Stakes at Del Mar, the yearlings were arriving for the 1966 Del Mar select yearling sale. As one might imagine, Mr. Harcourt was flying high. Again and again, he asked Pat and me what we had seen in the stables that interested us. He wanted to repeat his success.

It was some coincidence but Pat and I were standing not fifty yards from where we had first seen Bahroona when I caught a glimpse of a chestnut colt that blew me away. Was this possible—was this a magic place where perfectly conformed racehorses sprang out of the ground, right in front of my eyes? I held my breath and checked the catalog.

Once again the pedigree was modest but the conformation of this horse would add a point or two to the overall score I had given Bahroona the year before. He stood out like the glow of a gorgeous sunset, a copper red chestnut without a white hair on him.

Though the yearling wasn't on Pat's or my list for inspection, I approached the stable of Dr. Bart Baker, a respected California veterinarian, and asked him to show me this colt by What's Ahead out of Imbrosecco. Often a horse will catch your eye from a distance but, with close observation, you can change your mind, and that's exactly what happened then. I thought he'd been outstanding from a distance; up close, I considered him to be the best I had ever seen to that time. This gorgeous yearling had a triangle that was symmetrical as well as extremely well proportioned. If Bahroona scored 9 out of 10 for conformation and movement, this colt scored 9.9.

There is no question that it is better to create the foundation of a racing operation with horses that have a chance to succeed at classic distances of a mile or more. The world of international racing has a tendency to minimize the importance of the pure sprinter, and I thought that this yearling, unlike Bahroona, had the potential to produce strong racing ability over the classic distances.

In the world of buying horses, you learn to keep your opinions to yourself. You don't want excessive competition from other bidders, and there is a lot of work to do in the process of selection. You can't just like a horse and then buy him. If you're going to do a good job, you've got to study veterinary reports, X-rays and volumes of information about the performance of horses in your target's pedigree. The buyer who broadcasts his interests during the examination phase is generally less successful.

The fact is that I was smitten with this yearling, but I didn't want to be premature with my comments. I knew that Mr. Harcourt would get excited and try to affect my judgment, so Pat and I didn't tell him about the colt until just before he went in the ring to be sold. While Harcourt was excited about my impression of the horse as a physical specimen, he was quite negative about the pedigree. He went straight to his friends to ask their opinions. Their response was, "Are you crazy?!" I remember Mr. Harcourt saying that What's Ahead was a failing sire and that Imbrosecco possessed only sprint capabilities.

Not to be denied, I went to the ring and bought the yearling of my dreams. When the hammer fell at $5,000, Mr. Harcourt remarked, "Well, here we go again." If that were to be the case, it wouldn't be a bad deal. However, we wanted more than a Bahroona sprinter—we needed a horse capable of winning classic races if our operation was going to prove itself.

The yearling was among the first to be started on Flag Is Up Farms. We had transferred there straight away and the place was growing around us. He and about eighty other Thoroughbreds arrived around the first week in October 1966 to begin their careers as professional athletes on our new Solvang property. Sharivari was Mrs. Harcourt's choice of name this time, and I know of no good reason for it except that she liked the sound of it.

It was apparent from the outset that I had my hands on something very special. Sharivari was athletic but, more than that, there was something between those ears that set him apart from all the rest. He learned his lessons with a brilliance I hadn't known before, and soon he went off to the trainer Farrell Jones for his track work with a report from me saying that this one was the best I had developed to date.

Farrell quickly reported back that he had the same feeling for Sharivari as I did. He advised that we take our time with him because we might very well have a classic horse. We gave him only two races in 1967 and they were late in the year. In the first one he finished third and it was an easy trip. Farrell remained excited and explained to me that this was part of the young horse's foundation building. He asked me not to be disappointed. Within a month, Sharivari competed for the second time. Pat and I watched as he dominated his competitors and won with ease, serving notice that he was ready to go. He'd be a classic three-year-old.

In those days there was a gambling system in place that enabled people to bet on the Kentucky Derby from January of the year in question. They called it the "early book," and it was based in Tijuana, Mexico, because it was illegal to conduct such betting in California. When the early book was printed, Sharivari was the favorite for the Kentucky Derby, no less. My $5,000 yearling had been noticed.

The Santa Anita Derby is the West Coast stepping-stone to the Kentucky Derby, and two races lead up to it: the San Jacinto and the Los Feliz. These are internationally approved stakes races run on one of the toughest racing circuits in the world. In 1968 Sharivari won both of them. He was now the favorite for the Santa Anita Derby as well as the Kentucky Derby.

About ten days before the Santa Anita Derby I received a call from Farrell. He asked me to come to Santa Anita as soon as possible. I was there at five the next morning and Farrell escorted me to Sharivari's stall. While the groom held the horse, Farrell showed me a tiny little bump on his left fore tendon.

Yes, your blood really can run cold. Mine did right then and there at the sight of that little growth on Sharivari's leg. Farrell brought in Dr. Jack Robbins. I had known Jack for years; he was one of the very best racehorse veterinarians in the business. He was very clear and matter-of-fact.

"I can inject this small lesion with some cortisone and you might get through the Santa Anita Derby. What with the pressure of that race, though, I think you will not make it to Kentucky. Or we can stop racing him now and enter into a treatment program and I think you have a chance he'll come back fighting fit next year, as a four-year-old."

I was shocked. It took me five minutes or so to come to grips with reality. I was a professional and I knew that these things happened, but at that moment it seemed like the end of my world. I was totally drained.

The only option was to put the safety of the horse first. We stopped training immediately, and Sharivari was given the best possible medical attention in the hopes he'd come back about fourteen months later at Hollywood Park. The dream for the Kentucky Derby was broken, but we still had a wonderful horse with credentials to be a sire. Injuries to the major flexor tendons on a racehorse are devastating, but history shows that, with patience and diligent therapy, horses can return to win major races.

Sharivari came back as planned in 1969 at Hollywood Park. He was gorgeous and his legs looked as good as new. Once again, we all held out great hopes as he went to the starting gates for the Coronado Stakes. I watched him closely through my binoculars and he performed like a champion. About two hundred yards from the finish, with Sharivari two lengths in front, the Harcourts were up and ready to go to the winner's circle. Then I noticed him faltering slightly. He fought on gamely but finished third.

I went straight to the stable and remained with Sharivari through the cooling-out process. He wasn't lame and you couldn't detect a visible problem. Pat went home and I stayed overnight. I was in barn number three at about five the next morning when the groom stripped off the night bandages. There it was: that pea-sized bump was back, just as we'd seen at Santa Anita the year before.

With Bahroona and Sharivari both back at Flag Is Up, I strongly recommended to Mr. Harcourt that these horses be sent to New Zealand to become sires. While this was a far cry from the dreams of both Harcourt and myself, I believed it was the best way to go. Bahroona was a pure sprinter with blinding speed in his family, and while Sharivari could hold his speed for the classic distance, he was genetically a sprinter as well. New Zealand was the mecca for distance blood. The mares that would come to them were best at a mile and a half and up to two miles. It was my opinion that these two sires would put speed into New Zealand pedigrees and therefore be very popular. We made a trip and decided to lease a breeding farm called Alton Lodge near Te Kauwhata in the heart of horse country on North Island.

New Zealand had extreme quarantine requirements and after all arrangements were made, it was nearly a year before the pair arrived at the seaport in Auckland. We had secured the services of a New Zealand agent, Eric Hayden, to handle the business aspects of the breeding careers of our two stallions. Mr. Hayden was a wily character. He stood around five feet ten, was in his late fifties and had what I called an office body—that is, he was not physically fit. He was a chain-smoker, and he tilted up on his toes all the time, as if with that extra inch of height he could get more out of his cigarette. He dragged on it until it was burning his lip. Meanwhile, he had one hand in his pocket, constantly picking out the next cigarette from the packet.

Sharivari and Bahroona were taken directly to Alton Lodge and had settled in for a day or so when we got a call from Mr. Hayden. He said he liked Bahroona very much and believed he would be well received by the breeders for the 1970 season in the southern hemisphere. He thought Bahroona possessed near-perfect conformation for their purposes, and he'd already begun an advertising program for him.

As for Sharivari, Mr. Hayden thought he was the most beautiful horse he'd ever seen, with 100 percent perfect conformation. He went on to say that his legs were OK and if there had been a bump on a tendon, it certainly wasn't there now. He had already spoken with Colin Jillings (a champion Thoroughbred trainer) about the possibility of training Sharivari to race in New Zealand.

"Are you crazy?" I said. "We sent the horses there to breed. Don't even think of racing him."

I explained to Mr. Hayden that Sharivari had experienced tendon problems on two occasions. He was like a member of our family, and I didn't want to expose him to any potential further injury.

Mr. Hayden was disappointed. A race was coming up, the Telegraph Handicap, and he thought Sharivari could win it easily. If he did, he'd be one of the most exciting sire prospects in the country. I repeated my wishes that he be left at the stud to get his breeding career going.

About three weeks later the phone rang. It was Mr. Hayden, shouting as loud as his smoker's lungs would let him. "We won the Telegraph! Sharivari won by fifteen lengths. I've never seen anything like it!"

I could just picture him, up and down on his toes, pinching the last inch of smoke out of that cigarette.

I was stunned, speechless. When the shouting subsided I said, "If you want to remain in charge of this horse, get him back to that farm and get on with his breeding career!"

Mr. Hayden said that was no problem, he'd have a full book of mares now. He was sorry, but he'd just had to race him because the horse had looked so right in training. He promised me Sharivari would be back on the farm the next day.

About a month later, I got my next New Zealand call. Mr. Hayden said that Sharivari was training very well and had a great chance to win the Railway Handicap on the last day of December, if we wanted to enter him. They'd kept him in training just to retain his fitness for breeding, but his legs and movement were so fantastic, he wanted to give us the opportunity to try one more time. If Sharivari were to win, he'd be Sprinter of the Year for New Zealand and we could double the stud fee for the following year.

There was another option: the George Adams to be run on New Year's Day. Mr. Hayden said this race was at a classic distance and, if I chose it and he won, Sharivari would be Horse of the Year and triple his stud fee.

Mr. Hayden was incorrigible. I had the safety of the horse firmly in mind but felt I could approve the Railway, an easier sprint race. If he could be Sprinter of the Year, that was good enough.

We agreed by phone that Sharivari would be entered in the Railway and then go straight back to the farm, fully retired, to become—finally—a breeding stallion. I received my next call on New Year's Eve, 1970, and there must have been a hundred people screaming over the line. Sharivari was a ten-length winner of the Railway and the Champion Sprinter of New Zealand. There were shouts of congratulations and, while it was difficult to understand some of the accents, I knew that Sharivari was a hero.

Mr. Hayden told us how easy the race had been and how wonderful Sharivari's legs looked. He even told me they were watching Sharivari eat his dinner right then, while they made the phone call, and that he was an extremely happy horse.

"Wonderful," I said. "He'll be even happier when he sees a field of mares and the breeding shed on Alton Lodge stud."

Eric Hayden probably had two or three cigarettes in his mouth at the same time when he said something I never dreamed would ever emerge from any horseman's mouth. He wanted to race Sharivari *the next day*, and not just in any old race but in the George Adams at the classic distance.

"*No!* Not just no, but *hell, no!*" I cried. "That's not an option. Sharivari is to go to Alton Lodge and retire. Do not race that horse tomorrow!"

"OK," said Mr. Hayden. "It's your horse, you call the shots."

Sharivari winning one of his major stakes at Santa Anita racecourse, California

Twenty-four hours later I got my next telephone call: Sharivari had won the George Adams. An even bigger celebration was going on, and Sharivari was Horse of the Year in New Zealand for the 1970 season.

I had probably never been quite this perplexed. How can you want to choke a man and kiss him all at the same time? It was an incredible moment.

Sharivari finished sound and became a major sire throughout the southern hemisphere. Looking back, it's clear that veterinarians can be wrong, and obviously I came to a wrong conclusion as well. I had been intent on protecting the horse, and I suppose I might make that same mistake again. In Sharivari's case, those legs of his were a lot better than any of us thought they were.

All this happened thirty-four years ago, and if my career had stopped after Sharivari, I would still feel as though I'd been one of the most fortunate horsemen of all time. Sharivari was an incredible equine partner. Though he is now buried in New Zealand, the memory of him follows me wherever I go.

GLADWIN
AND ALADANCER

I n 1967, I was off to the major yearling sales in New York, Kentucky and Florida. It was time to get serious about the business of producing Thoroughbreds for high-level racing. I was happy with the results we'd achieved so far, especially with Bahroona, but I was setting higher goals for the future of Flag Is Up Farms. I was looking for exceptional physical individuals with pedigrees likely to be accepted by international breeders when the horses retired from racing. I was looking for bluebloods.

Pat and I made a trip to the Fasig-Tipton select yearling sale in August, which had been held in Saratoga, New York, for decades. Just as we had done for the Del Mar sales, we spent a lot of time researching the individual offerings and had reams of statistics about their families. We were looking at yearlings fetching more than $100,000 for the first time in our career. I hoped that my instincts as a hands-on horseman wouldn't desert me just because we'd traveled three thousand miles and were in a different world altogether, where blue blood ran deep in the catalog.

Mr. and Mrs. Harcourt flew in just before the sale began. Pat and I had been inspecting and studying for two or three days already and were staying at the Holiday Inn in downtown Saratoga. The Harcourts were booked in at the Gideon Putnam, one of the original five-star hotels of upstate New York. Saratoga was, and still is, a spa destination, but their high-class hotel, which even then cost hundreds of dollars per night, didn't offer a king-size bed. Mr. Harcourt, who was about six foot four, was accustomed to sleeping in one even though they weren't all that plentiful in the mid-sixties. I contacted the manager of the hotel and asked if I could arrange for one. The manager told me that that would be out of the question, that he'd never received such a request. I told him I'd get back to him.

Meanwhile, Pat and I managed to get someone from a good furniture store to agree to deliver a king-size bed to the Gideon Putnam Hotel. I called the hotel manager back and informed him that the bed was coming. He was insulted but allowed my arrangements to go ahead. The bed was duly delivered and the Harcourts arrived, unaware of the fuss. They settled in and were soon ready to be shown some of the yearlings.

You might wonder why I'd been so involved in seeing to the comfort of Mr. Harcourt. Was I an errand boy or a horseman? Well, I was a country boy who had a chance at entering the world of international horsemanship. I needed financial backing and Mr. Harcourt seemed to be the only one prepared to provide it. I had noticed his tendency to run hot and cold, and my attitude was if it took a king-size bed to keep his mood right, we'd get one. I was a survivor.

All of the sales sessions would be held in the evening after the races, and the four of us met on the sales grounds at about eleven o'clock on the first morning of the auction. We went down the book, showing the Harcourts the yearlings we thought were physically acceptable. After my first two years of selecting yearlings, Mr. Harcourt was very excited about the prospect of me choosing Thoroughbreds from a genetic pool far superior to that available in the California sales.

My wish list was quickly pared down to a handful of yearlings, and soon Mr. Harcourt realized that the one I really wanted was a bay colt by First Landing out of Dungaree. He was hip number 76 and bred by Mr. and Mrs. S. H. Rogers of Virginia. I told Mr. Harcourt that this yearling was the first one I had inspected at this sale that measured up to Sharivari.

First Landing was not a major international sire. Dungaree was from a good family but she had not performed well. Mr. Harcourt was considerably less than enthusiastic about the breeding but was willing to go along with me where conformation was concerned. The pedigree was far superior

Gladwin on a very special day in my career—the words on the picture tell the story.

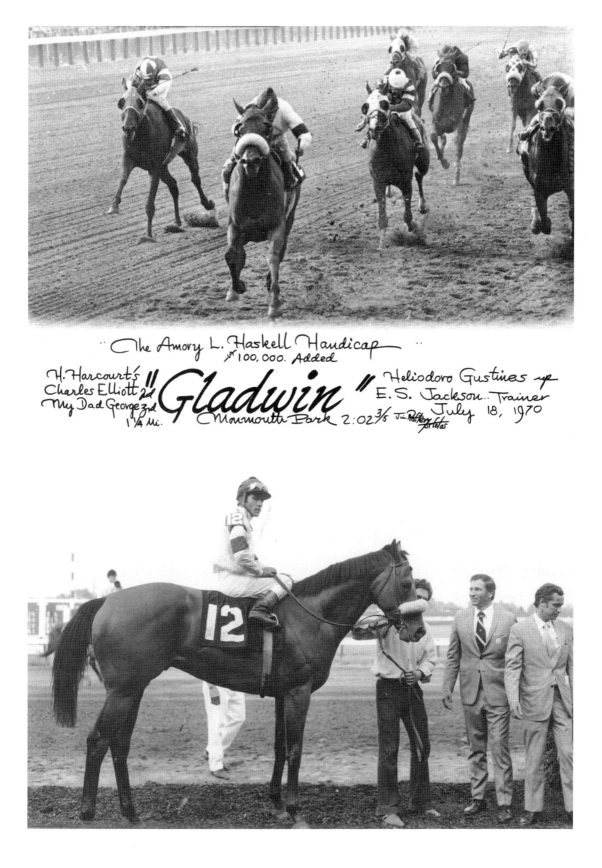

"The Amory L. Haskell Handicap
$100,000. Added

H. Harcourt's
Charles Elliott 2nd
My Dad George 3rd
1¼ Mi.

"Gladwin"

Heliodoro Gustines up
E. S. Jackson Trainer
July 18, 1970

Monmouth Park 2:02⅗

to Bahroona's and Sharivari's, but even so, it was not exactly what we had come here for.

We bought the bay colt that evening for around $30,000, and although I was the happiest horseman in town, I don't think Mr. Harcourt was too impressed. I remember him visiting his New York friends after the purchase and coming back to me with words of advice from each of them: the First Landings were unsound and Dungaree was too weak a mare to produce a high-level racehorse.

Mrs. Harcourt named our new yearling Gladwin. He was one of the first of the eastern purchases to go into training at Flag Is Up Farms. He was the highest-quality Thoroughbred that I had ever had under my tutelage to that point, and every aspect of his conformation was exemplary. I was determined to give him plenty of time despite his impatient owner, and did not race him at two years of age. He'd been having some trouble with shin splints (bucked shins) and from time to time his soles would bruise. He needed to be shod perfectly or he'd exhibit a slight tenderness. It took me most of his second year to correct these problems.

Eventually, I put him in training in California with Farrell Jones. As a three-year-old, Gladwin had two starts and finished second in one of the races. Mr. Harcourt was long-faced at these results. We'd spent a great deal of money and put a lot of work into Gladwin, and it didn't seem as though much was going to happen with him. I didn't have a happy owner on my hands, and I didn't seem to have an entirely happy horse either. I noticed the way Gladwin moved during his workouts and suspected that the hard tracks of California were stinging his feet. I started to think that he might need the more forgiving surfaces of the East Coast. I suggested we try him there.

While in New York, I had made the acquaintance of a young trainer by the name of Evan Jackson. He was a former jump jockey, five feet six or so, wiry and nervous as a cat on hot coals. He was always walking and talking and turning around and walking and talking some more. He was outspoken and gave his opinions quickly and fiercely. He was also a workaholic and knew the East Coast racetracks like the back of his hand.

Evan Jackson not only was good with his horses but had a very good jockey, Robyn Smith, who was working with him in the mornings and riding a few races. I knew her because it just so happened that she'd worked for us at Flag Is Up during our first year. I was a fan of this young lady; she rode well and, even more important, she had the ability to assess how a horse was performing. Robyn fell in love with Gladwin and guided Evan and me into a training program that would put him on course to perform at a very high level.

Gladwin won a maiden race at Belmont as a four-year-old, after which Evan and Robyn both suggested that we enter him in the Amory L. Haskell Handicap at Monmouth, New Jersey. I remember flying into New York and getting a shuttle flight over to Monmouth. I rented a car and, following Evan's instructions, drove to Colts Neck, New Jersey, to pick him up at a private airport. Evan flew his own Cessna.

He jumped out of the plane and slammed the door. "What ▓▓▓▓▓ are we doing here anyway?" he railed at me. "I got all the papers and tip sheets before flying over from Long Island, and we are 65 to 1 on the morning line."

Aladancer on the day of her victory in the California Oaks with me in a top coat

Any bet on Gladwin would get another two horses thrown in for free—that's what the experts thought of his chances. I was taken aback. All I could say was that we were there and we were entered, so we should just make the best of the day. Evan said it was a mistake to enter Gladwin in a major race with a $100,000 purse. We should have chosen a lesser stake to test his wings among the big boys. I drove to the Monmouth Park Racetrack with Evan ranting at me all the way about how stupid his recommendation had been and how I should never have gone along with it.

However, Gladwin couldn't read. He didn't know what a newspaper was and had never read a tip sheet. He'd never met a horse race betting expert, nor did he care what they thought. Gladwin entered gate number twelve but finished the race approximately ten lengths in front of the second-place horse.

We didn't have a big celebration because Evan and I were there by ourselves and he was rather unhappy at having been so wrong earlier in assessing Gladwin's chances. But I made a couple of phone calls home and I must tell you there was a tornado spinning inside me. This was a new high-water mark in my career with racehorses and one that will stick with me for the rest of my days.

I don't believe there's such a thing as good luck—you just have to be prepared to take an opportunity when it arises, and with Gladwin, that had taken a bit longer than usual. He was four years old before he won his first race, and I had had to learn to patiently stay the course during his problematic early years.

We went on to race Gladwin in the Hawthorne Gold Cup in Chicago that same year. The experts thought Gladwin would never have the stamina to stay the mile and a quarter; they were certain his breeding wouldn't allow him to achieve that distance. But once again, Gladwin proved the experts wrong. He won the $100,000 Hawthorne Gold Cup, finishing his mile and a quarter in 1:58.8, a new track record.

Meanwhile, Pat and I had returned to the Fasig-Tipton sale in Saratoga in 1969, still in search of a true blueblood that had the kind of conformation I preferred. Fresh from a lot of criticism about Gladwin's pedigree, I wanted to find a horse whose lineage would allow for running the classic distances but that also possessed the speed necessary to excel on American tracks. We found one: a chestnut filly as red as a desert sunset, looking as athletic as a yearling could. Some might have said that she was too short, both up and down and front to back, and I suppose they would have been right. But perfection is unachievable when judging conformation, and this filly seemed to be well balanced and symmetrical. The triangle that I look for to judge conformation was clearly visible and she walked with the grace of royalty.

When I looked at her pedigree page, my pulse rate really began to soar. She was by the legendary Kentucky Derby winner Northern Dancer, a gold-card-carrying blueblood, and out of Mock Orange, whose family tree read like the equine equivalent to the Kennedys'. Pat and I talked half the night about whether we could buy the filly the next evening.

When we were able to purchase her for $30,000, I was over the moon. We shipped her to Kentucky, where she joined some other yearlings for the trip to California. Named Aladancer, the filly was not all sweetness and light. She was aloof and slightly arrogant. She seemed to think that she was better than any of the other horses around her, and the fact is, she was. During training she seemed to be telling me, "Let me know what you want me to do, then leave me alone and I'll get it done for you. I don't want to sit around and visit. I want to perform."

Aladancer marched through her training and early races problem-free and then firmly landed in the world of big-time racing when she won the California Oaks. She was my first player on the national high-level Thoroughbred racing scene and earned $191,135 during her career.

As for Robyn Smith, she married one of the greatest entertainers of our time. She became Mrs. Fred Astaire and was a loving partner for him for the rest of his life. Mrs. Astaire has never lost her keen interest in horses and is often a visitor to major races throughout the United States.

MR. RIGHT

Gladwin taught me a great deal about the ideal conformation of a Thoroughbred racehorse and gave me the confidence to remain loyal to the impressions I formed in the early stages of examining and working with a young horse. He was also responsible for my acquaintance with Evan Jackson.

Shortly after I met Evan, Daniel Schwartz of Palm Springs, California, approached me and asked if I would find a good horse for himself and a friend. That friend was Frank Sinatra.

They were interested in owning a horse that could perform in high-level racing, and Schwartz advised me that, with his new partner, he simply couldn't take any chances. I would have to look for a horse that was an established performer because Mr. Sinatra needed something to be excited about right from the outset if he was to remain interested in the horse business.

I guess you could say I was motivated. I investigated leads from Florida to New York, out to Chicago and up and down the Pacific Coast. It was Evan who came to me one day and said I should consider purchasing Mr. Right for Schwartz and Sinatra. Mr. Right belonged to Peter Duchin, one of the most famous concert pianists of the time. The horse was already a stakes winner and had proven his worth on both coasts. I believe he'd already earned about $200,000, and he seemed to be sound and ready to continue his successful career. The danger was that if his performance tailed off under my management, it wouldn't look good for me. Horses can lose interest in racing, even without bad management, and I would be in the granddaddy of all fishbowls if it happened in this case.

I decided to take a chance and buy Mr. Right for Schwartz and Sinatra. Since Evan had been training the horse, I was pleased to leave him there with the idea of racing him in both New York and California. Though he was a relatively small horse, Mr. Right fulfilled my hopes in a very big way, and Schwartz and Sinatra had a lot of fun with him. He retired at the end of the 1969 season with seventeen wins and $667,193 in earnings, number eight on the list of all-time earners until then. I helped syndicate Mr. Right and he retired from racing to a successful breeding career.

I felt I had come a long, long way from riding Ginger and winning my first trophy at the age of four. I was a whole world away from rounding up mustangs on the ranges of Nevada and achieving join-up in the wild with Buster. But Mr. Right helped validate my theory that a horse is a horse. Their needs are similar, whether they're bluebloods or mustangs, and a good horseman should be able to judge their performance no matter what their calling might be. Mr. Right showed Pat and me that horses could take us places we never dreamed possible.

ROUGH FROLIC
AND CATHY HONEY

With Mr. Right's success, the excitement was palpable in the Schwartz-Sinatra camp. Pat and I were invited to Palm Springs for a party Frank was throwing to open a restaurant called Jilly's West. Jilly Rizzo was a lifelong friend of Frank and had moved to Palm Springs from New York so they could continue their friendship without having to travel so much.

As you can imagine, when Frank threw a party, it was a lot of fun. He'd invited about twenty friends and relatives on this particular evening, including his daughter Tina and Frank Jr., and his favorite piano player, Joey Bushkin. Frank sang a couple of funny little songs and tried to get others to perform, calling out the name of the next person at the table to take the mike. Dinah Shore sang, and seeing her was an incredible experience for me—I'd been a lifelong fan. Frank Jr. sang some songs and got everyone laughing with stories about his dad and the family. Jilly told a few jokes and stories of the old days in New York and New Jersey. Dale Robertson was another of the guests that night, an actor with whom I had worked many years before. He had been the star of the television show *Tales of Wells Fargo* during the 1950s. He was tall and handsome, but before that evening I hadn't realized what a great voice he had.

Pat and I were sitting near the end of the table. As Frank progressed toward us, I remember Danny Schwartz calling out, "Sing us a few songs, Monty. What's your voice like?" Frank spoke up quickly and saved me some embarrassment by saying, "You just keep producing horses like Mr. Right and you don't have to sing for your supper."

The party finished up with everyone around the piano while Mr. Bushkin played some of the most beautiful music I'd ever heard. It was an enchanted evening.

That night Pat and I were houseguests of the Schwartzes, and we accompanied them to Frank Sinatra's house the following day for brunch around the pool. Danny and Frank took me aside at one point and told me they were ready to buy another racehorse now that Mr. Right was retired. This time they wouldn't mind taking a bit of a chance, but they'd like a two-year-old that showed some ability. I asked what sort of price range they were thinking of, and they said price wasn't a concern; they wanted to shoot for a world-class performer.

By 1969 there was a new way to market young Thoroughbreds: as two-year-olds in training. The horses had to be ridden under racetrack conditions. While they weren't required to exhibit work at speed, the consignors often chose to go a sharp quarter of a mile or so in order to impress buyers. These sales began in Florida and were usually held on one of the major racetracks in that state.

I discussed the upcoming catalog with Frank and Danny and pointed out approximately twenty high-class colts in the 1969 sale of Florida breeders' premier two-year-olds in training. Frank asked me to sharpen my eyes and find him the best young stallion on offer, in terms of both conformation and pedigree.

Once again I was as motivated as anyone could be. Pat and I pored over the catalog for the upcoming sale, which was to be conducted at the Hialeah Race Course in Miami. I traveled to Miami alone in order to watch the training of the horses for about a week before they were actually sold. Arriving at the track around five each morning, I tried to get to know as much as possible about the individuals that caught my eye. Many of them were eliminated within a three-to-four-minute inspection. I wanted near-perfect conformation.

One chestnut colt impressed me from the first moment I saw him. He was in the consignment of Ocala Stud Farms Incorporated. The colt was by Rough 'n' Tumble, a leading Florida sire, and out of Individuality, a good mare from a high-class family. He was already named Rough Frolic and was one of the most impressive young Thoroughbreds I had examined up to that point in my career. I judged him to be right up there with Sharivari and Gladwin.

I called Frank and Danny and went over the page with them, explaining that I thought Rough Frolic might turn out to be the sales-topper. Many of the good horsemen there seemed to be paying a lot of attention to him. Schwartz and Sinatra both said that if I liked him that much, I should try to buy him. "What's my ceiling?" I asked. "Half a million dollars," they replied.

I tried to remain calm during the conversation but when I hung up the phone, I did my best Irish jig. I was walking on air. A half million dollars would have shattered all records paid for a two-year-old in training at that time. I was thirty-four, still quite green in my career, and here I was buying a half-million-dollar baby for Frank Sinatra. I rushed back to the stable area with my sights locked on Rough Frolic. I wanted to spend as much time as possible observing him throughout the daylight hours. I checked the veterinarians' reports closely; they were as clean as could be.

While I was standing near the entrance to the racetrack, a chestnut filly walked by on her way to a morning workout. She caught my eye almost as intensely as Rough Frolic had a couple of days before. Catalog numbers were displayed on the horse's saddlecloths, and I quickly opened my book to her page. Cathy Honey was her name. I saw she was by Francis S out of a mare called Honey Ration. By coincidence, Rough Frolic was coming from his stable at the same moment, so I could watch both of them on the racetrack at the same time.

Cathy Honey was probably the smoothest-traveling filly I had ever seen. She moved over the racecourse like a gazelle. She was elegant and feminine, but at the same time her muscular frame had a ruggedness that promised an athletic strength few fillies possess. Her pedigree was mediocre but I had fallen in love with her. When she came off the racetrack, I followed her back to her stable to watch the cooling-out session. I requested her vet reports and made my way to a pay phone in the barn area.

I called Danny Schwartz first and told him about the filly. I said that I needed more time to be certain she was everything I thought she was. Suddenly I realized I'd disturbed Danny from a sound sleep—it was only seven in California. He had his catalog on the nightstand beside the bed

Rough Frolic receiving one of his many awards on the way to ruling the
Hunter Division of US horse shows in the early 1970s

and Cathy Honey's page. I can only think it must have been the early hour that caused his reply to be so abrupt.

"Forget about it!" he said. "Are you crazy? You were sent to buy the best stallion prospect the sale had to offer, with sufficient quality to be accepted internationally as a sire if we are successful at the races. We told you we were willing to spend a half million dollars. Now you call me and recommend a filly that has a page that ought to sell for $10,000 or so. We're not interested in buying this sort of two-year-old."

I don't think I said ten words during what turned out to be a long conversation. I apologized for waking him and told him I wasn't suggesting Cathy Honey should be a replacement for Rough Frolic. I was calling because I thought I might buy her in addition to the colt. She seemed to be the same kind of athlete as Sharivari and Bahroona. I told him to forget the call and said I would get on with my work with Rough Frolic.

Yet I couldn't get the filly out of my mind. I called Mr. Harcourt, my partner in Flag Is Up Farms, and outlined the situation to him. He also advised me to adjust my thinking and give more consideration to genetics and less to the physical makeup of young Thoroughbreds. He said it was genetics that gave a horse the potential for breeding on an international level. However, if I could buy the filly for less than $15,000, he'd be interested in owning her just for the fun of winning some races—if she could.

I didn't get any sleep that night. When I arrived at the sales ring, I realized that every major personality in the Thoroughbred world was there and ready to bid. Very few people knew me at that point and I spent my time outside the sales pavilion observing the horses being prepared for auction.

Rough Frolic was the first of my two targets. The early bidding was brisk and it was soon apparent that he would be the sales-topper. Arnold Winnick, a Florida trainer, was my stiffest competition as bids passed the $200,000 mark. Toward the end, we were bidding in $25,000 increments, and I was ultimately successful at $350,000. Just to give you an idea of the kind of excitement that caused, the entire sale averaged about $50,000 for each horse that year. When a two-year-old fetched anything over $100,000, it was serious. A price of $350,000 was way off the scale.

Frank and Danny were happy when I called with the news but considerably less exuberant than I was. They congratulated me and said they'd discussed the pedigree with many of their racing buddies and felt that Rough Frolic fit their criteria. I explained my plans for shipping him by plane to California and assured them that I would ride with Rough Frolic to ensure his safety.

The press swarmed over me, wanting interview after interview. They went crazy over the fact that Frank Sinatra was to be a partner in this beautiful individual, bred in Florida by the state's leading Thoroughbred breeding operation.

As the minutes ticked away, I began to worry that my filly would be working her way toward the sales ring while I was standing there, answering questions. I managed to pull myself away from the pencils and tape recorders about five lots before her turn and raced out to the walking ring just as she was entering the staging area. She was a thing of beauty and yet practically no one was following her—unlike the throng that had chased Rough Frolic into the ring.

I tried not to show too obvious an interest in the filly. People now had their eyes on me and, while they were still trying to figure out who the heck I was, my interest just might stimulate an extra bid or two for this two-year-old daughter of Francis S. I looked at the other horses in the walking ring while measuring Cathy Honey out of the corner of my eye. She walked with a proud arrogance that spoke of championship quality.

Cathy Honey fetched just $12,500 and the sales ticket read, "Purchased by Monty Roberts, agent for Hastings Harcourt and Flag Is Up Farms."

I now had two horses to escort to California, and I was thrilled to be arranging for the air shipment of what I thought must be my future champions. The flight went without a glitch, and although I was exhausted when I arrived in Solvang, I kept Pat up for hours telling her about the experience.

Mr. Harcourt came by the following day and seemed pleased with Cathy Honey. Two days later Danny, Frank and Jilly Rizzo flew to Santa Barbara, where we met them for the drive to the farm. Jilly had purchased a pair of Sicilian donkeys a few months before as a Christmas present for Frank, and I had agreed to keep them on our farm. Jilly asked far more questions about the donkeys than Frank did about Rough Frolic.

We drove straight to the stable and put Rough Frolic on display for our three guests. Frank and Danny beamed with pride. As we watched the young horse, Frank told me that Danny had mentioned my early morning telephone conversation during their flight to Santa Barbara. He said he'd read in *The Daily Racing Form* that I had purchased Cathy Honey, and he was interested in seeing her.

My blood turned to ice. I realized Danny had not discussed the matter with Frank immediately after my phone call. I had thought that neither of them had had the slightest interest in her. I now tried to make light of the situation and agreed to show them the horse, a silly little purchase of $12,500.

Cathy Honey came out of the stable as proud and beautiful as she was in Miami, but still, she was a filly and no match for the magnificence of the young chestnut stallion. Frank had his catalog in hand and put his finger on the page under the name Francis S.

"Do you know who her sire is named after?" he asked.

"I've no idea," I replied. Then suddenly, the ice in my veins turned to permafrost. Francis S: of course.

I suppose if the sire had been called Francis *Albert* S, my feeble brain would have picked up the association. Now I realized the Florida-based stallion had been named after one of the greatest singers of all time, the man standing next to me: my new partner Francis Albert Sinatra.

"It's a sign," he said. "It's meant to be. I want to buy this filly, and if Danny doesn't want half of her, it doesn't matter. But I would very much like to have her."

I explained that not only had Danny told me to forget buying Cathy Honey, but he'd also said she wasn't the type they wanted anything to do with. I told him that after that telephone call, I had contacted Mr. Harcourt, who had agreed to buy the horse. She wasn't mine to sell. Frank said he understood the situation, but he asked if I could convince Mr. Harcourt to let him buy the filly.

We all made our way back to the house, where Pat had prepared a wonderful lunch. We ate outside, from a spot where we could overlook the farm and the Sicilian donkeys that were running and playing in a paddock just below the house. It was an unforgettable day, a beautiful memory for Pat and me.

After driving them back to Santa Barbara airport, I called Mr. Harcourt, who came up with a brilliant idea: he'd sell Cathy Honey to Sinatra, providing Sinatra would sell him a half-interest in Rough Frolic. However, when I made the call to Palm Springs, Frank said he wasn't willing to give up half of Rough Frolic, and the matter was put to rest.

Rough Frolic was trained on the Flag Is Up training track for about thirty days before we asked him for any speed. Prior to sale, he had been given two official breezes (speed drills); each of these sessions is logged in the books as three furlongs in 35.2—quite acceptable for a two-year-old in the early stages of training. A successful racehorse will eventually be required to better this by about a second, but there was plenty of time for improvement in our outstanding chestnut prospect.

I watched Rough Frolic almost every day and he was exactly as he had been in Florida: generous, easy to train and silken in his movements. I told my rider to give him an easy three furlongs, to allow him to choose his own pace. I wanted the horse to tell us what he wanted to do. Rough Frolic finished the three-furlong work in exactly the same time: 35.2.

We continued training on the farm for the next two or three months, allowing him easy regular works until his joints X-rayed as fully mature. In the early autumn, we shipped him to Evan Jackson at Belmont, New York. Evan had already seen Rough Frolic a few times but he called to say he was delighted with how the young horse looked. Evan was excited about the prospect of training another horse for Sinatra and Schwartz, particularly in light of the fact that Rough Frolic was such a high-class individual. Evan wanted to take his time with this youngster and target him for the classic races as a three-year-old.

I suppose it was about ten days or so before I got a report back from Evan on Rough Frolic's speed drill in New York. Evan said he hadn't pushed the horse and he went an easy three furlongs, finishing the drill in 35.2. We laughed. The horse had now worked three furlongs about ten times and each of them in 35.2. Evan told me this was just fine. No one should worry; he would improve.

A month or so later, Evan was growing a little concerned. He said that no matter what he did, Rough Frolic seemed to stick at 35.2. He was a one-pace horse. He looked good doing it, but it wasn't good enough.

The next months would prove Evan right. Rough Frolic never won a race in his entire career. I can only imagine how disappointed Sinatra and Schwartz were. I know how disappointed I was. I was the one who'd selected him and managed every step of his career. The question now was what we could do with this very expensive, highly bred, gorgeous individual, who moved like a champion but whose clock was stuck on 35.2.

Since my background had been the show ring, I thought Rough Frolic had the potential to be a strip hunter. This is a contest where the horse is judged on his style of jumping rather than on the height of the fence. At the conclusion of the jumping, the horse is stripped of tack and shown in hand, and the judge awards marks for conformation.

While this discipline isn't as famous as the Kentucky Derby, the horse-show world looks very favorably upon an exceptionally beautiful

Thoroughbred strip hunter. The event requires athleticism and beauty, and Rough Frolic had a full measure of each of those qualities.

We put him into training as a hunter and he immediately showed an affinity for it. He looked at the training fences as if he knew exactly what to do about them, as if he'd been a hunter in a former life, and he sailed over them with the ease of a gazelle. Professionals just couldn't believe he was a beginner.

We were able to sell Rough Frolic for around $200,000 to a California man who was prominent in hunter circles, Jay Lennon. The horse went on to become one of the best strip hunters the United States has ever known. He won championship after championship, enjoying a career that lasted about ten years. His success showed me how important it is to keep an open mind and search out the place a horse really wants to be. The talent was there. I simply needed to find the form it wanted to take.

Mr. Lennon was offered as much as $500,000 for Rough Frolic but he had such an emotional connection with the horse that he refused all offers. He eventually bought a farm property about ten miles from Flag Is Up and retired Rough Frolic there. I was able to see him many times afterward and he remained a beautiful individual well into his twenties.

Meanwhile, what happened to Cathy Honey?

She went into training with Farrell Jones at Hollywood Park in mid-1969. Unlike Rough Frolic, she always seemed to have another gear you could ask for. Farrell liked her from the start, but he had the distinct impression that she'd perform better in long-distance races than in the typical California sprints. He gave her a very easy two-year-old season, demanding very little from her in only a few races. She won one of her starts, coming from behind, which validated Farrell's opinion that she was a filly that wanted long races. She wintered well in preparation for the following season.

At the 1970 Santa Anita meeting, Cathy Honey won the Santa Ysabel Stakes. Once more she came from behind and won with authority. She came out of her race sound, and Farrell and I began to plan for her future. We both agreed that she was better suited to East Coast racing and thought she had a chance in the Filly Triple Crown, which was run in New York.

We made arrangements to ship Cathy Honey east and contracted the jockey Lafitte Pincay to ride her in the New York races. She went on to victory in the Acorn Stakes at Aqueduct; the Vineland at Garden State, New Jersey; and the Ladies Handicap back at Aqueduct. In that same year, she finished second in the Coaching Club American Oaks, the Mother Goose Stakes at Belmont and the Santa Susanna Stakes at Santa Anita.

Cathy Honey demonstrating why she was voted three-year-old champion filly of the USA in 1970

Cathy Honey won $196,146 in 1970 alone. That record placed her at the top of the three-year-old fillies competing in America that year. Jimmy Kilroe, senior racing secretary in the United States, voted her the champion three-year-old filly for 1970.

Though Cathy Honey had a very mediocre pedigree, nobody had told her that her father didn't really make it as a top-class sire or that her mother had failed to impress the world with her breeding. What Cathy Honey had, only God can give a horse. Her heart was full of generosity and she had the body to back it up. She took to race training like a duck to water and became a champion.

At the conclusion of her career, Mr. Harcourt received an offer for her for $350,000—ironically, the very sum that Rough Frolic had been bought for—and he just couldn't turn it down. In total, Cathy Honey brought a gross income of approximately $628,000 to her owner.

Rough Frolic never saw Cathy Honey race but if he had, I'm sure he would have been impressed with her beauty and ability. Cathy Honey never saw Rough Frolic perform as a hunter but I think she would have been impressed by him, too. Pedigrees and price tags wouldn't have mattered to either one of these equine champions. As the old saying goes, one should never judge a book by its cover. These two Thoroughbreds drove that lesson home to me in spades.

FANCY HEELS

Mr. Harcourt suffered from a manic-depressive condition and often behaved erratically in our business dealings. Pat and I were always ready for something to go wrong—we just never could have guessed how wrong. I described the following episode in greater detail in my first book, *The Man Who Listens to Horses*, but it's worth giving a short account of what happened here because it changed our lives dramatically.

In 1971, when I was thirty-six years old and we had already enjoyed some great successes together over a period of seven years, Mr. Harcourt said he'd like me to meet his psychiatrist. He wanted me to know about his psychological problems so that I might understand him better, and our relationship would be more likely to continue. He repeated what he often said: that our family meant the world to him and he didn't want Flag Is Up to go wrong for any reason.

I agreed to visit his psychiatrist, and he told me that Mr. Harcourt suffered from something called sand-castle syndrome. I'd never heard of it and didn't have a clue what it meant.

"If a child takes great pleasure from building a sand castle on a beach," the psychiatrist explained, "that pleasure is exceeded only by the excitement of watching the sea come in and destroy it." I suddenly felt dread to the bottom of my boots. He went on. "Mr. Harcourt has a pathological compulsion to build something up and then to make sure it's destroyed."

This was worse news than I could have imagined. What had I got my family into? Back at home, Pat and I looked out from our terrace. Flag Is Up Farms was spread out in the valley below us. It had everything that we could want: a training track, breeding barns, space for up to five hundred horses, the covered round pens, accommodation for staff and its own equine hospital. Everything was working. With Mr. Harcourt's help, we were on the way to gaining a world-class reputation. We had built one enormous sand castle.

Sure enough, the psychiatrist's words came true about a year later, and the tidal wave engulfed us. Hastings Harcourt turned up with a lawyer one day and said he wanted out of our arrangement. The lawyer was there to put this into effect in short order. I was in a hurry to get it over with, too—there was a decent chance any new owner would keep me on. Mr. Harcourt left the room and the lawyer took over. My hopes were raised as we discussed the terms. Everything seemed fair. I had a 5 percent ownership in the property and this was being respected.

Then came the bombshell. The lawyer said, "In addition to this, Mr. Harcourt has instructed me to tell you that he wants his riding horse, Travel's Echo, shot dead . . . and disposed of . . . He wishes you personally to shoot him, rather than have him go to another home. He also wants you personally to shoot Mrs. Harcourt's driving ponies."

Mrs. Harcourt had bought a pair of driving ponies but had never used them. We had kept them in good shape at Flag Is Up.

He then ordered me to shoot two racehorses, Veiled Wonder and Cherokee Arrow. Neither had performed well enough for his liking, and he felt as though they'd disgraced him.

We'd been telling ourselves to expect bad news but nothing like this—and it was to get much worse.

I went into a frenzy of activity; I certainly wasn't going to shoot any horses. I made some calls to close friends and within hours I had "sold" them, carefully logging the money into Flag Is Up accounts so that I couldn't be accused of theft. I agreed to repay everyone, so essentially I was buying the horses from Harcourt at their appraised value.

Things went well to begin with. Mr. Harcourt didn't realize what I had done. A buyer for the farm was found and plans were moving ahead. Then Mr. Harcourt began to stall, and we soon came to realize that the path he'd chosen would become a lot rougher for us. He wanted to destroy everything in sight. When he discovered that I'd saved the horses, he had me arrested for theft and thrown in jail. After I was freed, Mr. Harcourt became even angrier. The farm, the horses, our very lives were in jeopardy. We were told a contract had been taken out on us. Pat and I sent the children into hiding while we moved to a nearby farm. I even rode into the hills and camped out in hiding for a time. Meanwhile, Mr. Harcourt was selling off Flag Is Up Farms in lots, as fast as he could.

We were away from home for over a year, during which litigation flew in every direction. At the conclusion of it all, an elderly judge pointed at me across the courtroom and said, "I want to see that man smile." I loved that judge. A settlement was reached whereby Mr. Harcourt was obliged to sign over to us what remained of Flag Is Up Farms as compensation for his malicious prosecution. Though the property was significantly reduced, the core of it was still intact and we now owned it. We could go home.

With the changed circumstances, massive adjustment and restructuring were necessary if Flag Is Up was going to get back on track. We didn't have deep pockets, nor did we have the backing of a wealthy partner. Pat and I went to work with more resolve than we'd ever mustered in our young lives. The overheads were daunting.

It was 1972 and I had been out of show-ring competition for five years in order to run Flag Is Up Farms. After the crisis with Harcourt, I was tempted to go back to what I knew best and make another run at producing championship horses, particularly in the reining, cutting and cow horse competitions. The risks would be lower than with Thoroughbred racing and the chances of success higher. At the same time, it seemed foolish to waste the experience I'd gained in selecting and training some of the best Thoroughbreds throughout the late sixties. I was at a crossroads. As I have done so many times in my life, I waited for the horses to tell me which way to go.

Pat and I have raised forty-seven foster children. Some were with us for a short time only, some for many years. One of the girls who spent a large portion of her growing-up years under our roof was Sue Sparrow. Sue met

OVERLEAF *With John Wiester up, Fancy Heels shows his ability to control cattle, 1976*

Dave Abel at Cal Poly University while she was living with us and they were married in 1968. Afterward they moved to Elko, Nevada, where Dave became a prominent appraiser of the large cattle operations of the Great Basin region of the western United States.

I talked to Sue and Dave about going to the Elko Horse Show that year to look over the reined cow horses that would be competing. These were ranch horses that worked long hours each day for their cowboys. They were fortunate to work in a natural setting without the show-ring training that often leads to antipathy from horses. You often see excellent equine athletes with good work ethics and cooperative attitudes at the Elko competition. During the early part of my career, I saw many horses from this environment become very successful in the show rings of the western United States. I hoped to find such a horse to help kick-start the new Flag Is Up Farms.

At Elko I soon spotted a horse that impressed me. He was tall, copper red and very athletic. He had the body and coordination of a potential show horse, though his head was unattractive. I learned that his name was Fancy Heels, and I kept a close eye on him in the early competition. He looked like a classic mustang/Thoroughbred cross with a fair bit of feathering on his legs. His attitude about working cattle was like a border collie's about herding sheep. A little effort, I thought, could turn him from a good working ranch horse into a top-caliber show horse.

Fancy Heels won one of the preliminary competitions on Saturday, which earned him a place in the championships on Sunday. If I was to buy him, I hoped to do so before then. If he won, his price would surely rise. Dave knew the owner and told me his name was Randy Bunch, a buckaroo (ranch cowboy) who could always use the money. He introduced us.

"Well, he's for sale, all right," said Randy. "That's why I brought him to town in the first place. I didn't come here for the scenery, but I've got a good horse and I want some money for him."

"How much?" I asked. Randy paused for a minute and then raised his head, looked me in the eye and said $3,500. I was surprised but pleased by the low figure and immediately agreed to buy his horse. We shook hands and I wrote him a check right away. As I handed it over, I asked Randy if he was looking forward to showing the horse in the championship class the following day. Randy looked at me with a quizzical expression.

"You own the horse," he said. "You show him."

"Now wait a minute," I replied. "I've never even sat on him yet, and I don't have any clothes or equipment."

Randy crooked a finger at me and said, "I want to show you something."

We walked toward Fancy Heels's box stall and Randy ushered me inside. From underneath the bedding in one corner, he picked up a half-empty bottle of whiskey. He held it high between us to let the light shine through.

"That's how much whiskey it took to get me through the elimination classes. I don't intend to have to drink the rest of it to get through the championship. I came to town to sell him; I've sold him, and now I'm going back to the ranch. Good luck with him."

Dave offered to help me find all the equipment I would need to show Fancy Heels myself and tried to encourage me, saying he thought I had a good chance in the championship class. I rode Fancy Heels for an hour or so to get acquainted with him. He was well trained but I wasn't familiar with his movements or the cues one might use. The following morning, I rode him again for about half an hour, which was just enough time to get his muscles warm and to discover that he could trot at nearly twenty miles an hour—but not enough to figure out where all his buttons were.

Though I was ill-prepared to ride the horse properly, Fancy Heels and I won the herd-working phase of the three-part championship. The good score was encouraging but I knew that the herd work was his strength. We were acceptable in working a single cow down the fence, finishing second in that phase. Our dry work was the weak spot in our performance, but nevertheless we came second in the championship.

I was eager to get Fancy Heels home and start training him for world-class competition. I thought I could do it in a short period. But after a week of working with Fancy Heels, I had gained a lot of respect for Randy Bunch. I realized he'd brought the horse very close to his full potential. The changes I considered necessary to improve him were going to be much harder to effect than I had originally thought. He was a seven-year-old horse with well-established work habits and was already working near the top of his ability.

After a month, Fancy Heels was 10 percent less effective than he had been at the Elko show. I remember sitting down one evening and telling myself that I was a major producer of racehorses and the trainer of several world champion working horses. I told myself that I could get this job done. I just had to increase my efforts.

After four months of training, I realized I had made several mistakes with Fancy Heels. I had been asking him to go at *my* speed and to learn at *my* rate. I had failed to respect the years of work that had already gone into him. And I hadn't recognized his position on the matter. He was a cow horse and he wanted to work cattle. I decided to spend the time to get him back to where he'd been. If successful, I would attempt to market him to someone who could take advantage of his skills without expecting world-class performances in the show ring.

Once we began spending time with cattle, Fancy Heels and I had a lot of fun. I started to think that he might like team penning, an event that was just rising in popularity at the time. In team penning, horses work cattle very much as they would on a ranching operation. Fancy Heels became one of the best team penning horses ever and carried his new owner, John Wiester, to many wins.

So there's no such thing as failure. Failure is merely the point at which you have an opportunity to learn, and while I didn't reach the level I wanted for Fancy Heels, he was able to teach me some valuable lessons. There's an old saying: "Don't judge a man until you've walked a mile in his moccasins." I walked a mile in Randy Bunch's moccasins and found he'd done a very good job of optimizing Fancy Heels's potential. He wasn't a top show-horse trainer, and so I'd assumed I could easily improve his horse. But horses will often humble the best of trainers and, with the future of Flag Is Up resting on my shoulders, I experienced a healthy dose of humility. The incident was sobering and made me realize I couldn't keep my farm and family above water with show horses as our primary income. I needed to find a part of the horse business that we could afford. Thanks to Fancy Heels, I put my thinking cap on and formulated a plan.

PETRONE and HOLLINGSWORTH

Pat and I came to the conclusion that we had to get in gear and produce some Thoroughbreds worth their salt, or we would be unable to keep Flag Is Up Farms. We were running an operation with enormous overheads and needed cash flow—quickly. I could work with all the horses like Fancy Heels and start all the mustangs the world had to offer, but that just wouldn't get the job done. Yet we could no longer afford to take the high risks associated with investing in the world of bluebloods. Furthermore, we simply didn't have the money to do it.

We decided to explore the possibility of buying Thoroughbred yearlings to sell as two-year-olds in training. A yearling sale was coming up at Hollywood Park in October 1972, and we were interested in a colt entered there—consigned by Hastings Harcourt, of all people—whose sire was Petrone.

We knew this French-bred stallion well because we had managed his American racing, and later breeding, career. It's an interesting story. His owner was the actor Eddie Constantine, often called the French Humphrey Bogart although he was born and raised in the United States. Eddie enjoyed three decades of stardom in France. When he was in his sixties, he bought Petrone, a dark brown stallion by Prince Taj out of Wild Miss by Wild Risk. Petrone was raced lightly as a two-year-old, registering one win and one third. In 1967, at the age of three, he had seven starts with one win, two seconds and one third. The following season, Eddie entered

Petrone nine times but he won only two unimportant races. Eddie, slightly embarrassed by the mediocre performance, contacted Murty Brothers Agency in Lexington, Kentucky, with the intention of transporting Petrone to the United States and selling him.

I was contacted by the Murtys in January of 1969 and asked to inspect the four-year-old at Santa Anita racetrack. What I saw was a tall, lean, well-conformed Thoroughbred with the classical look of a European distance runner. Petrone stood about 16.2 hands and had a body frame that would impress any student of equine conformation. Nearly black, Petrone had a naturally frosted tail, a mixture of black and white hair that many would call salt and pepper. He moved with an elegant stride and appeared to have four very correct, sound legs. I read the veterinary reports and discovered that he had been given a clean bill of health.

Petrone was the type of horse that could cross with California sprint mares and bring to the offspring the ability to stay the classic distances of a mile to a mile and a half. With a price tag of $200,000, Petrone was an interesting prospect but a bit risky. Before making an offer, I contacted friends of mine in France who told me that, in their opinion, Petrone favored hard surfaces and races of a mile and a quarter or more. I recommended to Mr. Harcourt that we should try to buy Petrone for around $150,000.

Our offer was accepted and Petrone was put into training with Robert Wheeler. We went to work on a program to quicken his pace and targeted a series of classic turf races of a mile and a quarter to two miles.

The San Luis Rey Handicap at Santa Anita was target number one in my little plan to have a Group I winner stand at stud at Flag Is Up Farms. "Group I" is the term used for the highest grade of internationally approved stake races, just a notch below the classics, such as the Prix de l'Arc de Triomphe. Petrone came in second, performing better than I had seen him do in his French videos. He ran with a bit more speed, closed well and was beaten by one length, appearing to need slightly more distance.

Our next Group I challenge was the San Juan Capistrano Invitational Handicap at a mile and three-quarters. Petrone was an easy winner and thus became the Champion Turf Horse of the Santa Anita meet for 1969. We had purchased him in January and by April we had a champion and banked his

Petrone wins the San Juan Capistrano, Santa Anita racecourse, California.

purchase price. I was filled with excitement and felt there wasn't a horse in the world that could outrun Petrone on turf over a mile and a quarter.

The next goal we set for him was the Yankee Gold Cup Handicap at Suffolk Downs, near Boston. He ran with the utmost confidence but finished third in a large field after experiencing traffic trouble. I watched as the eastern jockeys built a trap for John Sellers, Petrone's regular jockey, and stopped him repeatedly as he tried to make his run in the last quarter of a mile. Those are the facts; I'm not trying to make excuses. I will always believe that Petrone was the best horse in the race.

The Group I Sunset Handicap at Hollywood Park in late July would be Petrone's final race. If he could win the Sunset at two miles, he would be the Champion Turf Horse for Hollywood Park and thus California for that year. This would send him off to stud in grand style. The best horses in America were there to compete for the $250,000 purse, but I was filled with confidence. Petrone's workouts since the Yankee Gold Cup had been outstanding and I thought he was by far the best in the field.

This time John Sellers took great care to avoid any traffic problems. He held Petrone out wide on the course, which meant he had to run a greater distance than the horses closest to the rail but ensured him a clear path if he had the stamina to overtake the leaders in the final three or four hundred yards. Petrone cruised along, sitting about eighth of twelve runners until they were in the final turn. Then John Sellers let out a notch on the reins and Petrone came flying into the home stretch, passing horses as if they were standing still. He opened about ten lengths on the field and won with his jockey standing in the irons, wearing a smile you could see from a mile away. There was certainly no need for a whip except to wave it in the air in celebration as Petrone crossed the finish line. He completed the two miles in 3:18.00, which was a new American record for the distance.

As a teenager I had run races like that in my head while I mucked out the stalls, playing the role of the racing commentator, talking it out loud, bringing horses across the line ten lengths in front and calling it a new American record. This time I had experienced the real thing.

Petrone was retired and began his breeding career at Flag Is Up in 1970. Now one of his offspring was going to help us keep our home and our lives together.

The colt's mother was Princess Pet, one of my blueblood purchases of whom I thought very highly. She had conformation that was among the very best of my female selections, and I was excited that we might have the chance to buy one of her babies. If we could make this purchase for less than $10,000, I believed we just might get him working well enough to sell six months later at the California Thoroughbred Breeders Association two-year-old in training sale. If we got lucky, we might get as much as $20,000 for him. We'd have expenses, but there was the possibility of some reasonable net profit.

With all this in mind, we went off to the October yearling sale at Hollywood Park, aiming to buy the colt. His name was Hollingsworth.

Pat and I examined him with great care and diligence. This was the first time we were venturing into the world of Thoroughbred ownership all on our own, and I must say it was daunting. We checked the veterinary reports and, with all our homework done, we gave the yearling very high marks as a racing prospect.

When Hollingsworth entered the ring, I don't believe that either Pat or I held out much hope that we'd be able buy him for less than $10,000, but we agreed that that was our upper limit. When we got him for $3,500 we were like a couple of kids who had just won a raffle. Only $3,500! How could you buy a good Thoroughbred horse for $3,500? We felt he was worth at least $10,000. We were young and invincible. There wasn't one moment when we questioned the wisdom of the purchase.

I had been watching some of the other yearlings, and while I was not in love with any but Hollingsworth, I felt that a son of Curragh King might be a good buy at $5,000 or $6,000. I ended up buying the chestnut colt, whom we called Country Rogue, for $1,100. Now that's crazy. You cannot buy a racing prospect for $1,100—but I did. With $4,600 invested in two horses, we went home to get our bones busy preparing them for their next trip through the auction ring in six months' time.

Pat rode Hollingsworth, and our daughters, Debbie, aged fifteen, and Laurel, thirteen, were often pressed into service as exercise riders. Both young Thoroughbreds trained well throughout the winter and came up to the March sale in impressive fashion. We were not back in the blueblood business, but I felt we had a very good chance of coming out with a good profit and paying some bills.

Country Rogue was the first of our two to go under the gavel and when he walked out of the ring, the price board showed $9,200. I suppose there were some embarrassed Thoroughbred breeders around when Pat and I did a war dance, celebrating the fact that we'd made more than we'd invested in both babies on the sale of just the one horse. Hollingsworth would further increase our profit.

As he was set to go into the ring, our pulse rates soared. I had asked him for three furlongs that day in an attempt to impress the bidders, and he had answered with a 34.1, the fastest time recorded by any sales horse. Hollingsworth now entered the ring sporting a brilliant, glossy coat. My long years of preparing horses for the show ring had paid off. As the handler circled him, the bids quickly racked up: $10,000, $20,000, $30,000 . . . $39,500 was the final bid. After they picked me up off the floor, I took the lead shank and walked Hollingsworth back to the stables. We had just topped the sale. For two horses that had cost a total of $4,600, we received $48,700. Pat and I were in business on our own and we were doing OK.

The journalists came running to the barn full of questions about how I had chosen this particular horse. I don't remember what I told them, and they wouldn't have known what I was talking about anyway. I liked his conformation and I loved his mother and father. What more was there to say?

Not only did Hollingsworth and Country Rogue sell well, but they ran well, too. Country Rogue was a good winner in California. Hollingsworth was the first winner from the 1973 two-year-old in training sale and was the first stakes winner from that venue. He was also the first stakes winner that Pat and I produced on our own—and from our first attempt.

Hollingsworth gave us the courage of our convictions. Our enterprise made sense. Others saw it, too. Several people approached us about investing in future purchases we might select. A gentleman from the San Francisco Bay area by the name of Chuck Wilson offered to be our new financial backer. We could ride the tide upward if we had good sales, but he was willing to take a large part of the financial risk if we didn't do so well. This would allow us to buy more yearlings and increase the size of our consignment, which would improve our chances of success.

Mr. Wilson was a great inspiration to both Pat and me. He turned out to be not just a financial partner but also a good friend. He would prove to be the wind beneath our wings as Pat and I took off on a twenty-year career as leading two-year-old consignors in the world of Thoroughbred racing.

From a business standpoint, the lesson Hollingsworth taught me might possibly be the most important any horse ever provided. Hollingsworth said, "If you think you can judge horseflesh, get some courage. Do it for yourself. Believe in your principles and work hard to maximize your potential." Hollingsworth set us up in business and I will be forever grateful to him for that.

AN ACT

With the money from Hollingsworth and Country Rogue safely banked and our agreement with Chuck Wilson in place, Pat and I purchased eleven yearlings for marketing in March 1974. We invested $93,172 and received $280,200. We were the number one sales consignor and had the highest-selling individual at $65,000. When expenses were figured in, we returned 66 percent per annum interest on a six-month investment. Everyone was happy.

The following March, we consigned thirteen horses that cost us $191,000 to buy and brought in $387,000. Our farm operation was growing and making increasing demands on our time, and so the following year Pat remained at Flag Is Up while I went off to Kentucky to restock for the season. For decades the Keeneland sales pavilion in Lexington had been the largest venue for Thoroughbred racing prospects worldwide. I signed for twelve yearlings, among them the last crop of the legendary Swaps. This stallion had died in 1975 and, since he was so popular in California, I invested heavily in four of his offspring.

One yearling that I noticed went through the sales ring at Keeneland but did not reach his reserve price of $10,000. The colt belonged to Claiborne Farm, the leading breeding operation in America at that time. The founder, Bull Hancock, had died a couple of years earlier and his son Seth was now president and general manager of the huge operation near Lexington. They raised many of the best horses racing has ever known, including Secretariat.

But while sound, healthy horses were the strength of the Claiborne operation, marketing yearlings was not. Their consignment looked ill-prepared when compared with the other yearlings, who were all in show shape and presented by experienced marketers.

Still, Claiborne's brown colt struck me as having great potential. He was tall, rangy and correct in his conformation but he looked awful. His hair was sunburned and he had less flesh than was desirable. I loved the way he

An Act triumphs in the Santa Anita Derby in 1976—a pivotal day in my career. Pat, draped in the winner's wreath, and I are in the center of the photo, surrounded by more than fifty An Act fans.

AN ACT WINS THE SANTA ANITA DERBY
SANTA ANITA, MARCH 28, 1976 8th RACE 1 1/8 MILES, 1:48
OWNER: KATZ, BRUN & ROBERTS, ET AL RONALD MC ANALLY, TR.
JOCKEY: LAFFIT PINCAY, JR. PURSE: $150,000 GUARANTEED
2nd: Double Discount 3rd: Life's Hope

moved and had a strong feeling about his attitude and the look in his eyes, one of which was surrounded by a ring of white, much as a human eye is. Old-timers believed this characteristic indicated a horse that was very difficult to handle.

It was early in the sale when he went through the ring, and I just could not bring myself to buy a horse in that condition. Standing out back where most of the professional buyers hung out, I remember feeling strongly tempted to bid for him, but my arm would just not raise itself. One of the reasons was the image of Pat in my mind's eye. Pat was, and still is, a fan of pretty horses. This brown colt was not only not pretty; in his condition he was downright ugly. As the bidding progressed, it became increasingly clear that the colt was not going to make his reserve. He left the ring and went straight back to the Claiborne barn, unpurchased.

I made arrangements to have my twelve horses shipped to California and left Lexington to get home and prepare for their arrival. They were due to make the trip about ten days after the close of the sale. As I flew home, I couldn't get the Claiborne colt out of my mind. I read his catalog page over and over. He was by Pretense. Trained by Charlie Whittingham in California, Pretense had been very successful on the California racing scene. If I bought the colt, the fact that his sire had been popular in the state would help me sell him in California, and it wouldn't hurt that the leading trainer of the time had guided the sire's career.

What struck me most about the catalog page, however, was that the dam, Durga, had produced two fillies that were currently racing and showing a lot of promise. They were both owned by one of the leading personalities in racing at the time, William Haggin Perry, and he was racing them in California. "What have I done?" I asked myself. A giant opportunity had leaped up in front of me and I had failed to put all the pieces of the puzzle together.

When I got home, I explained the situation to Pat, and of course she was concerned about the horse's condition. She questioned whether we could get him into shape by March and present him as an attractive package to potential buyers. In the end, though, she told me to trust my instincts and make the appropriate decision. I called Seth Hancock immediately.

"Ahhhh, some guy from Chicago called me and said he would give me $7,500 for him, and I believe I'm going to take it," Seth Hancock said. I felt my heart sink. I told him that if anything went wrong with the offer, I would like to be considered next in line to buy the colt. Seth said he'd call me if the sale failed to go through.

For the next two or three days I walked around the farm stepping on my lower lip. The guy from Chicago wouldn't pass up the colt. I was an idiot. I'd searched all year for a prospect like this and then I'd let him slip through my fingers. I'd been asleep at the switch.

Then Pat called me on the intercom at the training barn and said that Seth Hancock was on the phone. My heart was beating a mile a minute as I said, "Hello, Seth. What's up?" Seth told me that the man from Chicago had decided not to buy the Pretense colt. If I wanted him for $7,500, I could have him. I tried to stay calm as I told him we would be sending a check that day, and I arranged for him to be included with my twelve original purchases.

When the yearlings arrived, Pat was stunned by the appearance of the Pretense colt. She didn't, however, make a federal case of it. She told me that I had my work cut out for me and I had better get busy if I was going to produce a two-year-old we could be proud of come March. I told her he was a fixer-upper. He had his Wednesday clothes on but when we sold him, we would have him dressed in his Sunday outfit.

"He's a fixer-upper all right," she retorted. "You've just got a lot of fixing to do."

I decided to name him An Act—it's the dictionary definition of "pretense." There was another reason why it suited him, apart from his sire's name. He was an incredible handful, and every day he challenged me with one act or another. He often behaved more like a mustang than like a beautifully bred Thoroughbred. I remember trying to introduce him to a stable blanket one day. As I approached him with it, he assumed a defensive stance and moved to the back of his box stall. I held the blanket up toward his shoulder and asked him to settle down. Snorting, he reached out with his left forefoot in one swift movement and knocked the blanket right out of my hands. One of my helpers had been watching and said, "He doesn't have that white around his eye for no reason." Still, his training went well for the first month or so.

When I start babies in late September, it's often not until the first of

December that I let them canter. I'm a firm believer in lots of trotting for young racing prospects before their bones are mature. When An Act began to canter, it was not a pretty sight. I had been very happy with his trot throughout October and November, but his canter was completely out of sync.

By January, I was still worried, but his two half sisters, Sarsar and Mama Kali, had moved well up the ladder in California racing and were both looking like top-notch prospects. I began to ask An Act for some speed, and it was then that I stood stunned by what I saw. When he put his body in overdrive, everything began to operate at peak efficiency. He began to look the part, too. His coat was glossy and his muscles seemed to grow day by day. I've often thought that speed is the most beautiful look of all for racehorses. By the time we got to Hollywood Park in February, my palms were in a sweat because I realized An Act was a very special individual indeed. In addition, he knew it and would constantly look for ways to act up, scaring me to death. There was no malice in him; he was just a baby full of energy. The champion jockey Lafitte Pincay made the trip to Hollywood Park from Santa Anita one morning to give An Act his workout, and he was full of praise for my brown colt.

The bloodstock agents began to appear. I was offered $50,000 and then $60,000, but we were entered in the sale and I was determined to let the public set his value. The day before the sale there was a preview of all individuals on the track and I decided to allow An Act to breeze three furlongs with my regular rider, Hector Valadez, in the saddle. An Act and Hector completed the three furlongs in 34.0, a new record for a sale of two-year-olds.

The agents followed my colt back to the barn, and I turned down $80,000 from a bloodstock dealer called Albert Yank. He was known as Alberto Pie the Good Guy, a dyed-in-the-wool horse dealer. His motto was "I'll stand on my head, till my ears turn red, to sell you a horse." The fact that someone so sharp was prepared to offer such a high figure to try to stop An Act from going into the sales ring was a good sign.

Our other two-year-olds had done well in the preview workout, but as you may imagine, Pat and I were intensely focused on An Act. At six the following morning, An Act's groom, John Flowers, took him out of the stall for a thirty-minute walk on the lead. He was jumping through his skin the day after his first serious work and, through no fault of John's, got loose while I was watching him. He ran like the wind, circling barn number three at Hollywood Park. I ran in the opposite direction and met him around the back of the stable. He came up to me with his tail straight in the air, blowing through his nose. I took the lead and brought him back to John for twenty minutes more walking. This time we kept him in the shed row where he was more contained. His antics had scared us beyond belief, but he didn't get a scratch.

That night he looked beautiful as he entered the ring. The three furlongs he had run the day before proved his athletic ability. Somebody opened the bidding at $50,000 and it sailed by $75,000. The offers slowed down after $80,000, and the auctioneer went in increments of $2,000 all the way up to $100,000. I can still feel the excitement as I recall the moment he was sold. The price set a new record for California two-year-olds.

Albert Yank was the one who bought him after all. He'd put together a group of clients to form a small partnership to buy the horse. As if fixed on his price of $80,000, Mr. Yank asked me if I really thought he was worth the $100,000. I told him I did. With that he said, "If you're so sure, take $20,000 off and you'll own 20 percent of him." I agreed but told him that if I was to own 20 percent of the colt, I wanted to be his racing manager. I wanted to make the decisions about his career if I was to invest to that extent. Mr. Yank agreed and An Act came home with us to prepare for autumn racing.

We decided to send him to the trainer Ron McAnally in September with the idea of racing him at the Oak Tree meeting at Santa Anita in October. I made everyone promise that this would be a schooling race and, regardless of the outcome, we would not ask for another outing until he was three.

Lafitte Pincay was booked to ride An Act. I was as nervous as I'd ever been in my life as I followed the horse from the stable to the receiving barn. He was like a playful puppy, dancing along on his toes and completely unaware that he could be seriously injured if he got loose or slipped and fell. I was scared to death that something might happen to him before we got him saddled.

As we left the receiving barn to go through to the saddling paddock, An Act jumped and played and struck out over the lead, getting loose from his handler. He ran across the lawn near the walking ring right through the throngs of racing fans. After jumping two park benches, An Act made a U-turn and came running back in my direction. He actually came to a sliding stop right in front of me and I caught the shank, leading him the rest of the way to the saddling paddock myself.

An Act was the perfect student going to the starting gate. He broke well and won his first start by about twelve lengths. His time was outstanding for a maiden starter. There was no question that we had an exceptional young horse on our hands and I began to plan for his 1976 racing season. I scheduled one more non-stake allowance race for January and then looked at the races leading up to the Group I Santa Anita Derby, deciding on a path often taken by derby prospects: the Santa Catalina Stakes in March followed by the derby in the first week of April.

An Act won both races. Obviously, we had great hopes for the Kentucky Derby a month later. But unfortunately it just wasn't to be. An Act developed a viral throat infection a week or so after the Santa Anita Derby and the organism attacked his left retinoid—a flap that closes the opening to the lungs when a horse swallows. He recovered but he'd never have the same ability to breathe. His racing career was over.

I was devastated. There was a world-class performer inside this young horse but we wouldn't see his full potential. In many ways, I felt very little responsibility for his achievements. All I did was help him to love racing and do it because he wanted to, not because he was forced to.

However, we had our Group I winning racehorse, and with earnings of $212,950 we looked forward to his career at stud. He was syndicated for breeding at a value of $600,000.

If Hollingsworth opened the door to the world of buying Thoroughbred yearlings, An Act escorted us through. A $7,500 yearling reaching the level of a world-class derby winner was unheard of in the mid-seventies. An Act did it in grand style.

ALLEGED

Approximately six months after we sold An Act, I returned to the Keeneland sales pavilion for the 1975 presentation of yearlings. I was confident that An Act, who by then was two, would become a superstar, but confidence by its very nature is fragile in the racing business. I needed to find horses selling well below what I perceived to be their fair market value in order to make a profit on them in just six months. Low prices were sometimes achievable because horses were not properly prepared, or because a snowstorm blew up, keeping buyers away. But the best consignors in the world were conditioning these yearlings, and since it was early September in Kentucky, we were not likely to have the snowstorm.

Pat and I met with our investors before I left California, and we agreed that, while we should move our sights a little higher, we had to keep our average cost well below $15,000. In order to accomplish this, we concluded that we should not pay more than $30,000 for any one individual.

Pat stayed in California while I made the trip to examine the horses and visit potential buyers. After making my initial round of the consignments, I was convinced that the average sale price would probably be around $60,000. It was going to be very difficult to find acceptable yearlings within our budget.

I spent a significant amount of time around the consignment of Lee Eaton. Lee was a friend of ours and a consistent producer of high-quality yearlings at both the Kentucky and the New York sales. While I watched his yearlings being shown to prospective buyers, a colt caught my attention, not because he looked well but because he looked awful.

Scanning his catalog page, I found he was by Hoist the Flag out of Princess Pout by Prince John—world-class parentage. I noted his present owner was one of the most prominent breeders in the United States, Mrs. June McKnight. I asked Lee about the colt, and he said he was doing the best he could to present him for Mrs. McKnight but that he'd had a lot of problems getting him to the sale. Lee explained that the colt had been very ill with an infected navel hernia. Surgery had corrected the condition but his recovery had cost him dearly in body condition.

An Act had looked rough when I bought him, but the shape of this individual made An Act look like a subject for an oil painting. The colt was probably 175 to 200 pounds underweight and every rib was clearly visible. His hair was turned inside out and was dull as could be. Still, I was immediately struck by the fact that this yearling had a triangle that was desirable in the extreme. Its base was as long as I had ever seen and its symmetry was perfection, which was not difficult to see because every bone was discernible.

Could I buy this colt, take him back to California and let Pat see him? She hadn't made a big deal out of the condition of An Act the year before, but this time there'd be a strong enough cause for justifiable homicide. I put a low score on the page of the Hoist the Flag yearling but wrote that he had the best triangle I had ever come across. I also wrote that I wasn't sure how valid the triangle was because I had no experience in judging one so visible because of ill health. I put him aside and went about my business.

As I recall, I purchased six horses and arranged for them to be sent to California to join the five I had already bought that year. When Mrs. McKnight's colt went through the ring, he was gaveled down at $30,000, but I learned later that he went back to Lee Eaton's stable unsold—shades of what had happened with An Act the year before. I went by Lee's consignment in an attempt to convince him to advise Mrs. McKnight to send him to California so we could sell him in the two-year-old in training sale for her. Lee knew that Mrs. McKnight wouldn't want to do that, but he did say she would be willing to sell him on the basis of half down and the other half after the sale in California. While the offer was tempting, I thought we would have to come up with $15,000, and I had only $10,000 left in my purchasing account. Lee said that he would accept $10,000 down and the balance after the in-training sale. Now I was really tempted, but I soon discovered that Lee was referring not to the $30,000 that was reached in the ring but to Mrs. McKnight's minimum price, which was $40,000. This meant that I would have to come up with $30,000 after the in-training sale.

I had just six months to transform the horse from awful to excellent if we were ever going to succeed with the purchase. I told Lee I needed to sleep on it, but I had the groom lead the colt for me once again. He was an outstanding mover. His stride was impressive and he cruised over the ground like a Rolls-Royce.

I didn't get more than two or three hours' sleep that night, alternately buying the yearling and reselling him very successfully, and then catching hold of myself and deciding I should tell Lee that I couldn't possibly accept the deal.

Alleged as a two-year-old in 1976

I went back out to Keeneland at about six o'clock the next morning and watched as they took the thin, bay colt from his stable to the van that would transport him back to Lee's farm. I examined him closely as he walked the two hundred yards to the loading dock. He appeared calm and cooperative as he loaded onto the truck—a difficult task for a young horse. It was this final inspection that made up my mind. I returned to the stable to tell Lee I would take the colt on the terms he'd suggested. The problem now was how to prepare Pat for the shock of her life. Our investors might also take a dim view of my selection, but it was Pat I was most concerned about.

When the yearlings arrived at Flag Is Up, she was stunned beyond belief. I was, too, because while the trip from Kentucky to California always sets a yearling back some, this one didn't have any cushion to fall back on. I walked him straight to the horse scale and he registered only 649 pounds. The other yearlings averaged about 950 pounds.

Pat questioned why we had invested in such a challenge. I remember she squared up to me just outside our horse clinic and said, "That's the last time you're ever going off to a sale by yourself." She was concerned that this particular purchase was going to derail the outstanding start we had made in selling two-year-olds in training.

It was Pat who came up with the name Alleged. The fact that he was by Hoist the Flag had her playing with the word allegiance, and she eventually applied for and received Alleged. I went to work, first to get him strong enough to accept saddle and rider and then to go through the starting process. Join-up, my secret weapon, was a complete success. We began to build a sense of trust. As he became stronger, he seemed to take charge of his own existence. Initially quite meek and passive, he seemed to grow psychologically as he gained in stature. At the same time he took to the environment at Flag Is Up very well and soon reached a weight of about 750 pounds.

Trotting is a very important part of the process I use for preparing young horses. It allows for the development of aerobic fitness without putting great pressure on the joints. Alleged trotted for approximately ninety days before I asked him to canter, nearly thirty days more than the average yearling. By January 1, he was around a month behind the rest of the babies but was gaining ground rapidly. He was up to about 950 pounds and was even growing in height, standing nearly 15.3 hands. I was encouraged but still

scared to death that I wouldn't even get the $40,000 necessary to recoup the purchase price.

Early in January we had a houseguest by the name of Billy McDonald. Billy was an Irish bloodstock agent who was visiting to observe our consignment as they trained. He intended to select one or two of our best yearlings for some clients based in Britain. We'd just received our copy of *Decade of Champions*, illustrated by Richard Stone Reeves. While Billy was reading it, he noticed that Alleged was the offspring of two individuals included in that publication. He flipped to the entries for Hoist the Flag and Princess Pout and told me that I had a rare individual in my consignment.

Billy hadn't yet seen Alleged and I was extremely nervous as I took him to the stable the following morning. If Billy liked the horse, he might recommend him to clients who could afford the high price I needed. Obviously, the challenge was to present Alleged in such a way that would please Billy. The horse was cantering by this time, and I must say that his athletic movement overcame many doubts about his general condition. I asked Hector Valadez, who had done a great job of riding An Act the year before, to present Alleged, and he did so in a very pleasing way.

During lunch, Billy told me he was impressed with the Hoist the Flag colt and wanted to see more of him during the next week or so. Before leaving the farm toward the end of January, Billy seemed to be confident that he could find a customer for our Alleged.

By the time the mid-March two-year-old in training sale took place, Alleged weighed well over 1,000 pounds and was very impressive as he negotiated the racetrack at Hollywood Park. Billy McDonald had appeared on the scene about a week before the sale and requested that I refrain from giving Alleged any speed drills. His clients would be interested only if no pressure had been put on his immature joints. I agreed because I didn't feel the horse was ready for speed drills either.

However, I was concerned. In an auction sale you need two bidders to elevate the price, and buyers might think there's something wrong if there isn't a speed test to measure the horse by. If the buyers' confidence was

First past the finishing post in the 1978 Arc

reduced by our lack of a speed test, I was likely to get just one bid over my reserve. This worried me, but I had given my word and that was it.

Alleged came up to the sales ring looking very well, and there seemed to be good interest in him, speed test or no speed test. I had put a $49,500 reserve on him, which would give me nearly $10,000 to cover expenses after the purchase price—a breakeven sale.

The bidding started at $25,000 and the auctioneer was calling for $50,000 when I saw Billy McDonald raise his hand. I nudged Pat and said, "We've done it." Then I heard the auctioneer calling for $75,000 and heard one of the bid spotters yell out, "Yuuup."

"Who was that?" Pat asked.

I said, "I don't know. It came from the other side of the ring." I couldn't believe what I was seeing as Billy McDonald signaled another bid at $100,000. With that I jumped out of my seat and moved to a position where I could see who was bidding from the other side. Pat followed me.

The bid spotter was beckoning to a man I knew from Colorado, Hoss Inman. He was in the habit of buying two-year-olds at very reasonable prices for racing at secondary tracks. I almost fell over when I saw Hoss signal a bid at $125,000. Billy came right back with a bid of $150,000, and after what seemed like an eternity, Hoss called out $160,000. The auctioneer asked for $175,000, and Billy responded with another bid. Hoss shook his head, got up and walked out of the pavilion. Pat and I walked over to Billy to congratulate him as he signed the ticket.

I asked Billy who the buyer was and he told me it was Robert Sangster of England, along with two or three other clients. I inquired who would train him, and he told me Vincent O'Brien of Ireland would. I had known Vincent for many years and was happy that Alleged would go to one of the world's leading trainers.

We gave our staff a party that night, and I remember saying a lot of nice things about the job they had done to bring along Alleged so beautifully. Pat and I got to bed about midnight but neither of us slept for more than two or three hours. This time, however, our restlessness was out of joy rather than concern.

The phone in our hotel room rang about six thirty in the morning. It was Billy McDonald. He was in trouble. Robert Sangster had cleared him to pay only up to $150,000. He'd got carried away when he went to $175,000. Billy asked me if I would take $25,000 off Alleged's price with an agreement that, if he should go to stud, I would be entitled to two breeding rights (shares) in him.

I quickly thought it over and decided the risk was too great. We needed to keep our operation afloat, there were enormous operating costs at Flag Is Up, and racing was an uncertain business. Alleged might never win enough to earn the right to go to stud, and if he did, he would probably stand in Europe, which would make it very difficult for us to use the breeding rights. I would also have to explain to our investors where the $25,000 had gone. I told Billy that I simply couldn't do it. With that, he said he thought he could talk Mr. Sangster into accepting the full price, which he eventually did.

When Pat did the recap of the consignment that included Alleged, it read as follows: twelve yearlings purchased for $170,000; twelve two-year-olds sold for $503,500. With expenses included, this amounted to a profit of over 350 percent per annum on a six-month investment. We were ranked first as consignors by gross sales and had the highest-selling individual, Alleged at $175,000, a new record price for a California two-year-old in training.

Alleged was shipped to Vincent O'Brien's Ballydoyle stable and began training immediately. Word soon reached me that Vincent was very pleased with Alleged and he was planning to give him plenty of time to mature. Alleged was given one late start as a two-year-old and won easily. He was allowed the winter off to prepare for the 1977 racing season, during which he'd be asked to compete against some of the best three-year-olds in the world. Alleged certainly measured up to the task, winning four races before being sent to France for the Prix de l'Arc de Triomphe.

Many Americans think that the Kentucky Derby is the most prestigious race in the world, and the Brits feel the same about the English Derby. The fact is that the Prix de l'Arc de Triomphe was, at that time, by far the most important race in the industry. This race is open to horses of all ages, and so three-year-olds are not often entered. But Alleged had impressed Mr. O'Brien and his owners so much that they decided to give it a try.

Alleged won, becoming the world's leading racehorse for that season. When the news came through, Pat and I were thrilled. This was as good as it gets. When we thought back to the start we'd had with him, it was an awesome feeling.

In 1978 Alleged made three starts and won all three. It was a record-breaking year for him. In the last start of his life, he once again won the Prix de l'Arc de Triomphe and was judged to be the world's champion Thoroughbred racehorse. Alleged's lifetime racing record reads: ten starts, nine wins and one second with earnings of $623,187.

Immediately after the 1978 Arc, it was announced that shares in Alleged were set at $400,000. Within ten days all forty shares were taken. If I had accepted the two shares offered to me, I would have earned $800,000. I kicked myself.

The Alleged syndicate eventually purchased Walmac Farm in Lexington for the purpose of standing him at stud. I went there many times to see him during the course of his breeding career and I often wondered if he remembered his old boss. Did he remember join-up? Did he remember all the good food and exercise we gave him to help him recover? I had had to practically become a professor in equine nutrition in order to improve his underdeveloped body in six months.

Alleged had an outstanding breeding career. Jockey Club statistics show that, along with his championships in racing at three and four years of age, he was the leading broodmare sire for 1998. He remained on Walmac until his death in 2001 at the age of twenty-seven.

They tell me I should be retired at my age, maybe fishing or lying in a hammock somewhere, but horses such as Alleged still excite these old bones and keep me going. They've given me so much, I can't think of retiring. My passion for horses won't go away. Each of the horses included in this book has been a powerful contributor to my career, but somewhere down inside me is the feeling that Alleged shone brighter than most.

NAPUR

In 1978 I bought a colt by Damascus out of a mare called Lodge for $50,000. Pat named him Napur, which is a region near Damascus, and he was a very attractive light chestnut with lots of white on his legs.

I was unable to sell Napur as a two-year-old in training as I'd intended, because of an infection called "scratches" or "dew poisoning," which he'd contracted in those beautiful white legs of his. So I took him home and eventually concluded that he was not likely to withstand the rigors of racing. His tendons and ligaments were swollen much of the time because of the infection, and it would be unfair to ask those legs to perform at ultra-high speeds.

My veterinarian, Dr. Van Snow, happened to be a fan of show-jumping. We decided to school Napur to determine whether he might be suited to that discipline. He soon let us know that he was quite comfortable jumping fences. His ability to measure his steps and gain elevation was quite extraordinary for such a young horse. We started to get serious about developing his career.

Napur began to win baby show-jumping contests immediately. As I recall, we were only about five or six months into the competition phase when Van came to me and said Hap Hanson was interested in showing him. Hap was, and is, one of the leading professional show-jumping riders in the United States, and while his interest didn't mean we had a champion on our hands, it was an encouraging sign.

Ridden by Dr. Van Snow, Napur shows his perfect form over the Grand Prix wall.

Van accepted the responsibility of continuing Napur's training and was soon taking him to some relatively major shows. Hap rode him and our team moved up the ladder of competitive show-jumping. After a year they were winning contests ranked at the top of the California circuit.

In his second full year of competition, Napur was competing at Grand Prix level, which placed him among the top two or three hundred horses in the United States. Van suggested sending Napur to Scandinavia and Europe for the following season. Will Simpson, another top show-jumping rider, was planning a tour of the major horse shows there in 1985 and very much wanted to take Napur, along with three other horses.

Agreeing to go for it, we shifted into top gear, and Van got Napur into the best condition possible over the six to eight months allocated to preparing for the junket. Napur was very successful on his tour east of the Atlantic Ocean and came back to Flag Is Up as one of the most promising show-jumping stallions anywhere in the world. His ability in the show ring, along with his impeccable pedigree, set him up to be well received as a breeding stallion. It was because of those two primary factors that we sold Napur. He eventually went to a show-jumping partnership for a price of $550,000.

Pat and I felt an extremely strong sense of accomplishment. Though it had taken a long time, and we had had expenses along the way, Napur's ultimate sale was more profitable than that of any of our other yearling pur-chases for that year. He is one more piece of evidence that good horse-manship and patience are often partners in success.

Napur helped broaden my experience in the horse industry in a sig-nificant way. Show-jumping people probably see me as a racehorse man; racehorse people view me as a Western show-horse trainer; and Western show-horse people would most likely say that I am an ex–rodeo cowboy. I really don't care how human beings view me. My only concern is how horses see me.

THE MUSTANG MARE

Throughout my career I had been secretly using join-up as a technique for communicating with horses and developing a relationship with them based on trust. The round pen at my former training establishment, in San Luis Obispo, was across a creek, well away from where anyone could see it. At Flag Is Up, which was crowded with horses and staff, the covered round pens had been built with solid tongue and groove sides. There wasn't a crack for anyone to see in. Any riders or horsemen around the place would have assumed I was exercising a horse in circles. It had become my habit never to mention it.

By the mid-eighties, I had started literally thousands of babies using join-up. After forty years' experience, the technique had become predictable and extremely effective. Domestic horses would normally join with me and follow me around with their noses at my shoulder in about ten minutes. Within fifteen minutes, they would be willing to stand for the first saddle of their lives. A rider was usually on their backs in an average of thirty minutes.

Like snowflakes, all horses are different, but when you come to know the true nature of these flight animals, the similarities far outweigh the differences. Barlet, for instance, had been a very aggressive horse, and although I had had to be very careful while doing join-up with him, the procedure changed him dramatically. For Johnny Tivio, on the other hand, perhaps the most important horse in my life and therefore left until the end of this book, join-up was vastly different. It was as though someone had asked him to come and join the party and instantly things began to take shape. With Bahroona, Sharivari, An Act and Alleged, I came to realize that join-up was allowing me to create horses that did their work because they wanted to, not because they were forced to. Isn't it true that we humans do our best work when we're doing it because we want to? I believed that my technique was giving me an advantage over other trainers. But I was keeping the knowledge of join-up from the rest of the world only because I felt they simply didn't want to know about it.

One day, as I was starting a baby in the round pen, some men were working on a tree that had been damaged by a storm about twenty yards away. Farrell Jones, who was visiting, lifted himself up in a hydraulic hoist parked near the round pen. As chance would have it, he could see directly into the pen. I wasn't aware he was there, but he could see everything that I was doing.

Farrell was puzzled—and certainly surprised. When I came out he asked me what was going on. He wondered if he could believe his eyes. I found myself telling him the basics about my technique, not without some sense of dread. His interest increased and he wouldn't leave me alone about it.

Accustomed as I was to rejection and disbelief when it came to join-up, my instinct was to keep it under wraps. Yet at the same time I longed to tell everyone. I was convinced I had discovered something that could transform the relationship between mankind and the horse forever.

Farrell wanted to tell other people about what he'd seen.

"Hell, no," I said. "That would get me into no end of trouble."

He asked me to give a demonstration for invited guests but I refused. He told me that I had something truly important to show to the horse world, and while I agreed, I felt that the rest of the world didn't want to know. He said it was my duty to give a demonstration. I couldn't argue with that—I did feel a sense of duty about it. In my heart I knew that join-up was something I should share, but I didn't want to risk it. The time always seemed wrong to bring it out into the open. I was afraid of jeopardizing my successful career in Thoroughbred racing. I didn't want to be regarded as a kook. I told Farrell that a demonstration wouldn't be good for business. He thought the opposite, that nothing but good could come of it.

"You'd think so," I replied, "but that hasn't been the case so far."

In the end he persuaded me. He organized a demonstration to which he invited the notable horse people of the area, as well as journalists. The event went very well, and I had a raw young Thoroughbred accepting his first saddle, bridle and rider in about thirty minutes. Articles about my technique appeared in various horse publications, and a lot of people talked about it. Others came to watch. I built a ramp up to a viewing gallery around the outside of the round pen, so now people could see in. Interest in what I was doing began to grow.

At the same time, however, business at Flag Is Up Farms slumped, falling by a quarter. I didn't have the heart to tell Farrell, but things were happening just as I thought they would. Apparently many trainers didn't understand my concepts, and what they didn't understand frightened them. They backed away. But change was in the wind and I could either fight against it or go with it. As usual, the horses were what carried me.

Around this time, I experienced an episode of join-up that must rank as one of the most extraordinary pieces of communication between species of all time.

I received a call one day from a lady who had just adopted a mustang mare from the Bureau of Land Management. The mare had a foal at her side that was approximately five months old. The new owner had heard about the work I was doing—perhaps she'd read one of the articles. In any case, she wanted me to start her mare. She intended to ride her and later pass her on to her children. I advised her to wean the foal first, and when they were well separated, I would put the mare through the starting process.

Ten days or so later, the lady arrived with her mare. She backed her trailer up to my round pen and released one of the wildest animals you could imagine. She told me the only interaction the mustang had had with humans was when they had brought feed and water to her. As I watched the mare, she seemed a daunting challenge. She was circling the pen, mindful of every sound around her and skeptical of every movement. She moved about the enclosure like a large wild cat.

Eventually, I entered the pen. I decided to take my time and give her all the space she needed. There was no hurry. The mare gave me all the signs of communication and was soon taking steps toward me. After about forty-five minutes I was touching her, and by the two-hour mark I had a halter on her and was leading her around. I could pick up her front feet but when I tried to pick up the back ones she kicked with fury. Soon I could rub her body on both sides and she would volunteer to stay with me, not taking the slack out of the lead rope.

In just over two hours, I indicated to my rider, Sean McCarthy, that he should bring in a saddle, bridle, saddle pad and another long line. While he was doing this, the mare was hovering very close to me at the south side of the pen. Sean left through a gate on the north side, closing it to leave me alone with the mare.

I started to walk toward the equipment Sean had placed in the center of the circle, and the mare began to follow me. But as we took two or three steps from the south wall, she passed me like a rocket. Running as fast as she could, she crashed into the saddle on the ground and started ripping it to shreds with her teeth. It was as if Sean had brought a lion into the middle of the pen and she had to kill it or die herself.

I froze in my tracks. The air filled with bits and pieces as they flew off the saddle. I was terrified I'd be next on the menu and started moving to my right, staying as close to the wall as I could. I was aiming to get around to the door on the north side and out of the pen.

Moving as smoothly and rapidly as possible, I'd made it about halfway to the door when the mare broke away from the saddle and ran straight at me. I was still about forty feet from the gate—too far to run. I fell to my knees next to the wall and balled up on the ground in a fetal position, covering my head with my hands. Sean was on the observation stand near the gate and I remember he jumped down into the pen just as the mare reached me. I was certain she would attack me, just as she had the saddle. She slid to a stop just over me, virtually covering me with dirt, and I got ready for something that wasn't going to be pretty. Her feet ripped at the ground, throwing clods of dirt on me. The noise was deafening and I prepared for bolts of pain to start shooting through me. But instead the noise subsided and the pain failed to occur. I don't remember even being touched by one of those flying feet.

Balled up on the ground, I could see the mare's head out of the corner of my eye. Her nose was near the wall in front of me and her hind feet were doing a dance near my toes. She was actually right over top of me when I

THE QUEEN MOTHER'S FILLY

A
fter the public demonstration of join-up at Flag Is Up Farms, Her Majesty the Queen, a keen horsewoman and racehorse owner, happened to read about it in two magazines, *The Blood-Horse* and *The Florida Horse*. Intrigued, she instructed her equerry (horse manager) Sir John Miller to get in touch with me and investigate my claims. Sir John telephoned a friend of his in California, a certain John Bowles, and asked him if he'd ever heard of this character Monty Roberts.

"I've known him for fifteen years and he lives five miles down the road," John Bowles replied, and he offered to contact me. When he called and said the Queen of England wanted to meet me, I thought he was joking.

Not long afterward, Sir John Miller came to see for himself what I could do, and we arranged a demonstration especially for him. At the time I happened to have several young horses in training from D. Wayne Lukas, a leading trainer of Thoroughbreds in the United States. Sir John watched as I used join-up to get a saddle and rider on a number of them. He was very excited by what he'd seen and told me the Queen would certainly be inviting me to come to England and to give just such a demonstration to an invited audience. Sure enough, in February 1989, Pat and I received an invitation to Windsor Castle for April of that year. Her Majesty's staff would arrange for horses and a round pen while we would provide a rider, Sean McCarthy.

I wrote about my first and subsequent visits to Windsor Castle in my first book, but there was one horse there who particularly stood out, and I must include her story here. She was a brown filly owned by the Queen Mother, and she was responsible for ushering in a whole new era of my life.

I arrived at London Heathrow on a Saturday morning to be met by Sir John. Pat, our son, Marty, and Sean were coming the next day. Sir John took me directly to Windsor and soon we were walking through the fields just below the castle, overlooking Windsor Great Park. The Queen's riding horses were grazing, separately, in small green fields of about two acres. A larger field, near the main gates of the park, held fifteen head of assorted breeds and colors. These were the horses that had been brought in from royal breeding farms for me to work with. Sir John told me they would eventually be carriage horses, ceremonial horses and possibly even officers' mounts.

As we wandered farther from the stables, we came to a small field where a filly was playing on her own and calling out to the others in a large, nearby field. Sir John told me she was a Thoroughbred from a sire and a dam that were important in the world of steeplechasing. "She belongs to the Queen Mother," he said. The plan was to begin with this filly at nine o'clock on Monday morning, and he hoped that the Queen Mother would be able to attend.

We discussed the schedule as we walked back to the stables. I said I would like all the horses to be led up to and through the riding school and the round pen the following day, Sunday, so they would be at least slightly acquainted with the trip and the environment. Sir John agreed this would be done. He told me the Queen was having lunch with Mikhail and Raisa Gorbachev but that Her Majesty would be available to welcome me the following morning and discuss the upcoming week. We went back to Shotover House, near Windsor, where I was a guest of Sir John, and retired for the evening.

We were back on the Windsor grounds at eight the next morning. With the help of some grooms, I set about bringing the horses to the riding hall for a walk through the round pen. The Queen was out riding and I was introduced to her on her return. The experience was overwhelming but she immediately put me at ease. She asked me about the wire-mesh round pen and suggested it looked a little like a lion's cage. In fact, I'd never worked horses in a pen of this type, but it would certainly allow the audience to see what I was doing. I felt I was in the presence of a good student of horsemanship, who was genuinely interested in what I did. While I never lost sight of the fact that she was the Queen of England, we were able to converse freely because my visit centered on horses and my concepts of working with them. More than twenty subsequent visits have proved that my first impression of the Queen as a true student of horses was valid.

Sir John told me that the Queen would come to the first demonstration, which would be with her mother's brown filly, but that her appointments would make it impossible for her to attend for the rest of the week. Arrangements had been made to videotape each day's demonstrations so that she could watch them in the evening.

Monday morning was glorious. Blue skies with big white clouds ushered in a day that Marty, Sean, Pat and I would remember for the rest of our lives. By nine o'clock, two hundred guests, including many dignitaries, had gathered near the round pen in the riding hall. The Queen, Prince Philip and the Queen Mother invited Pat and Marty to watch with them from a private viewing room. Having been introduced to the Queen Mother, I stood with Sir John Miller by a large door at the end of the riding hall. Everything was ready for me to enter the round pen with her filly.

My heart was racing a mile a minute and my adrenaline level was off the chart. It suddenly struck me that my work could not go well while I was in this state. I always tell my students to keep their pulse rates low and adrenaline down because horses will tune in to them. If we have high pulse rates, they will too. How in the world could I live by my own advice under these circumstances? Through a fog I remember Sir John introducing me to the audience, then leaving the round pen and clicking the latch behind him.

As soon as I removed the lead and released the filly, she quickly moved away. I suddenly calmed down. I think my muscles and some portion of my subconscious brain took over at that point and automatically performed the procedures that four decades of experience had taught me. Obviously, I had never worked under these circumstances before. Somehow, the presence of the Queen Mother was more daunting to me than that of the Queen, Prince Philip or the guests and dignitaries. I suppose, as a professional horseman, you tend to seek more than anything else the approval of the owner of the animal you are working with, no matter who else is present.

Through the grace of God and a filly that seemed to know how important this demonstration was, I managed to get through a good join-up, and she accepted her first saddle, bridle and rider. Sean appeared to be quite calm and did a great job despite the high-pressure environment. The filly quietly followed me around the pen after the saddle was removed and clearly demonstrated her acceptance of my nonviolent technique of starting horses.

I kept an eye on the door through which I expected to see the royal family emerge, as well as Marty and Pat. The Queen was the first to appear. With her right hand extended, she warmly approached me and said that my demonstration was extraordinary. Her Majesty had clearly been affected by what the last half hour had shown. Although I was totally uninformed about protocol with the royal family, I was now feeling relaxed.

Prince Philip was the next to appear. He walked briskly toward me, grabbed my hand with the strength of an athlete and slapped me on the shoulder with a firm gesture of approval. He asked me if I would work with some of his driving ponies that week, and of course I agreed.

For a moment, everything seemed to stand still as I awaited the owner. The Queen Mother emerged with Pat following. The emotion she showed surprised me. I noticed a tear as she reached out her two hands to greet me. I took both of them, as she said it was one of the most wonderful displays she'd ever witnessed. Instinctively, I put my right arm around the Queen Mother's shoulders. The security people stiffened and stepped forward and I was suddenly aware of what I was doing. According to etiquette, one never touches a member of the royal family. I quickly removed my arm and moved back, but Her Majesty continued to squeeze my left hand and, obviously moved, stepped closer to me. She told me to continue my work to bring about a better relationship between humans and horses for as long as I could.

At the gate of the round pen, the Queen Mother shook Sean's hand and thanked him for his part in the proceedings, while rubbing her filly's nose. The Queen, Sir John, Pat and I escorted her to her car. As we returned to the riding hall, I thanked the Queen for the time she had given me that morning and said I hoped she would be able to watch the videos of the rest of the week's work. Her Majesty replied that, with her schedule so packed with appointments, the videos were the only way she would be able to see

A work day for the Queen, the Queen Mother's filly and me in the riding hall, Windsor Castle, 1989

it. She went on to say that at the conclusion of the week, Sir John would assist with arranging a tour for me to demonstrate my methods throughout England. The tour would include twenty-one stops. It was quite clear that the Queen of England had enjoyed my demonstration and wanted other English horsemen and women to see it.

Back inside the riding hall, we took some pictures with the Queen Mother's filly and mingled with the guests before going off to lunch at the Savill Garden in Windsor Great Park. As I posed for pictures, I began to recognize the filly's importance to me. The Queen had just asked me to do a tour, and of course I had agreed. It was only later that I learned how rare this type of endorsement is. She also gave her approval for an article and photograph to appear in *Horse & Hound* magazine. Michael Clayton, then the editor of the magazine, was one of the guests, and he wrote the article himself.

Pat and I didn't know it at the time, but adjustments were being made to the Queen's schedule so that she and Prince Philip could come to watch the afternoon's demonstration, and she was present for almost eight hours on each of the five days I worked at Windsor Castle. I managed to start more than twenty horses during that time, and the Queen told me I must write a book to tell the world about my concepts. The Queen Mother's filly was ridden each day, and on Friday her royal owner returned to see the beautiful young Thoroughbred carrying her rider, Sean, calmly through the Windsor gardens, accompanied by the Queen's stud groom at the time, Roger Oliver, who was riding a trained horse.

Not long afterward we visited each of the cities on Sir John's schedule and completed the tour by May 18, returning to Windsor Castle with a report of events. I wrote a book, as the Queen had suggested, and more than any other one element, *The Man Who Listens to Horses* altered the course of my career and my life.

My relationship with the Queen has remained strong over the years, and I was invited to attend her fifty-year jubilee in May 2002 on the very grounds where it all began, back in 1989.

The Queen Mother's filly in Windsor gardens, Sean McCarthy up, accompanied by Her Majesty, the Queen Mother, our son Marty, myself, and Pat

Sure, there are important horses in my life, world champions and high performers of every sort, but the Queen Mother's filly was a fulcrum. My life changed direction and I found myself becoming a writer and educator, touring the world to demonstrate join-up. I often think back to the skepticism and disbelief I suffered as a child and the shadow it cast over the next forty years. That shadow has now been lifted. Join-up has met with a level of acceptance I could never have believed possible, and the Queen Mother's filly started it.

STANLEY

The California Thoroughbred Breeders Association discontinued its agreement with Hollywood Park, and from now on, the major California two-year-old sales venue would be the Pomona Race Track, about fifteen miles east of Santa Anita. Previews would be conducted at this half-mile track with virtually every entry being asked to gallop one-eighth of a mile. Selling two-year-olds became a different game entirely, and Pat and I were not prepared to push babies to perform one furlong in ten seconds. For nineteen years our consignments had led the world in producing two-year-olds prepared for racing, but now our lives were obliged to take a different path.

With join-up finally coming out into the open, I developed a missionary zeal about educating as many people as possible. At the same time, more and more people were requesting that I use my experience to help with remedial cases. Owners and trainers around the world wanted me to deal with specific problems that had beset their horses. So I moved into the next phase of my life: I became a traveling horse psychologist.

Horse & Hound magazine asked me to conduct some all-day teaching clinics at Stoneleigh Park and Towerlands, equestrian centres in England, and once again I went to see the Queen. I came away from that meeting keenly aware of her desire for me to conduct a demonstration tour in Ireland. During that trip I would meet another horse that would carve a permanent notch in my memory. His name was Stanley, and he was a three-year-old

Irish draft stallion. For various reasons he'd become very aggressive and extremely dangerous.

A member of the Queen's staff asked me to telephone Hugh McCusker of Lurgan, near Belfast, who would organize the tour. When I got him on the phone, he was doubtful and quite reticent. He told me that a lady had talked to him by telephone and said some things that seemed quite bizarre—something about communicating with horses and causing them to accept their first saddle, bridle and rider in about thirty minutes. Hugh McCusker went on to say that he wasn't interested in getting involved with "hocus pocus" stuff. He told me that if I wanted him to represent me on a tour of Ireland, I would have to go to Belfast and convince him there was good reason to consider the effort.

Though I was surprised by the conversation, I had faced this kind of skepticism for most of my life and knew I could answer it. I boarded a plane for Belfast, where a driver picked me up at the airport and took me to the McCusker home. Hugh is a big man with sandy hair, bushy eyebrows and a handshake that would crush steel bars. He sat me down in his living room, put me through a serious session of questions about what I might show people and expressed grave doubts that my approach would work.

Hugh said that Irish horses were much tougher than those in England and that my claims seemed outrageous. He announced that he had set up a little test for me involving a horse recently rescued from an abusive environment. He said I could back out if I wanted to, because the horse was no pushover. I agreed to his test and we drove to an indoor riding arena about twenty miles away.

About fifteen to twenty people were waiting when we arrived, and they brought in a thin gelding about five years old with a large open gash between his eyes and down the bridge of his nose. When I asked what had happened to the horse, his handler told me that he'd had an argument with a blackthorn limb. Hugh explained that this meant the horse had been hit with a kind of club. The poor creature was frightened and needed a friend. I had a rider on his back in less than thirty minutes. Join-up seemed to relax the fragile horse and give him a sense of safety. All I can remember Hugh saying is, "Full marks. I give you full marks. You're going on tour." Hugh's background was in producing show hunters, and he was the master of the hounds in his part of the world. He had great confidence and a flamboyant personality, and he had put me through a test as only a good Irishman could.

Roughly twelve cities were included on Hugh's schedule, spread out from the top to the bottom of the Emerald Isle. One of the last stops was a town just outside Dublin called, ominously, Kill. This is home to one of Ireland's most famous horsewomen, Iris Kellet. She'd recently sold her original training center to the president of the Irish Draught Horse Society, Fenton Flannely, and he apparently wanted my event to serve as an open house to the community.

The plan was to start two of Fenton's Irish draft fillies that had never been ridden. He said they'd have a coffee and cake reception afterward, where I could meet people and answer their questions. I agreed to this slightly different format. We arrived at the facility at about two in the afternoon.

The event began at seven thirty that evening, and with an introduction and a bit of time between the two fillies, I had both of them comfortably ridden by just after nine. During coffee and cake, Hugh mentioned that Fenton Flannely was very impressed with what he had seen and would be very happy if I would work with one more horse after the refreshments. I asked Hugh if he thought the five hundred people in attendance would want to stay after ten o'clock for another demonstration. He thought a lot of them would go home, but this last horse was mostly for Fenton.

As soon as word got back to him that I had agreed to work with his third horse, he made an announcement over the public address system: "Monty has agreed to work with my three-year-old stallion, Stanley. As you all know, he's never been saddled or ridden, and if any of you would like to stay after the coffee, you're welcome." People started to whisper and I sensed a feeling of excitement running through the audience. I asked Hugh what was going on but I don't recall getting a satisfactory answer.

When the audience was seated once again, it was apparent that more people were there than before the coffee break. I didn't understand how we could have an audience grow after ten at night. Hugh said he supposed this horse was of interest to them, and maybe they had called family and friends, encouraging them to come see me work with Stanley.

"Yeah," I said. "That's what I'm thinking, too, but I'm not so sure it's because they think he's wonderful. I have a feeling they sense some real drama here."

From a very early age, I'd attended jackpot ropings and match races and been exposed to every trick that horsemen play on one another. I didn't need a newspaper to tell me what was going on. The community knew this horse and it was probably not because he was a lovable teddy bear. What had I let myself in for?

When my late-night subject arrived, he had two strong Irish lads leading him, one on each side. They were followed by one of Fenton Flannely's trainers, Ronnie McComb. The lads had long leads, each one with a chain over the horse's nose. The fearful expressions on their faces told a large part of the story: they knew they were bringing Hannibal Lecter himself into the building, and he wasn't wearing a muzzle. The horse was moving left and right, challenging each of his handlers and resisting passing through the gate. From time to time he'd snap his ears back on his neck, showing how angry he was.

The boys carefully turned him loose and I knew this large chestnut had an appetite for human flesh. With the lads outside the pen and the gate closed, there was silence, which was odd considering there were now nearly six hundred people watching. Fenton Flannely took the microphone and told the audience I was going to work with Stanley. He said that the horse had been a champion when shown in hand, but that not much had been done with him for the past year.

As Fenton spoke, I watched the beautiful Irish draft horse circling the pen, intermittently walking, trotting and cantering. I could easily see why he was a champion in hand. He had a strong set of legs and a body that was balanced and symmetrical. His muscular neck and beautiful head indicated that he was probably more intelligent than his handlers wanted him to be. He moved with a grace and strength that were almost frightening to watch.

With my lapel mike open, I asked why nothing had been done with him for a year. Fenton Flannely answered that the horse had become a bit of a handful the last time he was shown, and they'd decided to leave him alone for a while in the hope that he would become a little friendlier toward people. I inquired whether they thought the time off had worked, but I don't think I got a response to that question.

With Stanley standing at the far side of the pen, I went in through the small gate and stepped a couple of paces toward him. He flew into a rage, pinned his ears flat on his neck and ran straight at me, mouth open and teeth exposed in a great imitation of a Bengal tiger. You could hear a collective gasp as I made it out of the gate and closed it just in time. Stanley came to a stop just at the other side of the fence and began to pace like a cage-bound lion. "Holy, moly!" I called out to my audience. Stanley walked back and forth inside the pen, moving his ears and snapping at the wire mesh.

I sat down on a chair next to my equipment bag. I will never forget the next few minutes because, whether these Irishmen knew it or not, I was very concerned for my safety. There's no doubt in my mind that if my health insurance agent had been there that night, he would have cancelled my policy on the spot. I relaxed for a minute, trying to think of a course of action. I thought of the newspaper articles that would appear the next day telling of either my great failure or my great success, or possibly there would just be a long list of injuries to a fifty-four-year-old Californian who thought he could handle a difficult Irish horse. Deciding to buy another minute or so, I had a conversation with the audience.

"What the heck are you trying to do to me?" I inquired. "I'm an old man. I retired from the rodeo arena twenty-five years ago. Five of my vertebrae are welded together. I'll be killed if I go in with this equine carnivore. Surely, the nice people of Ireland wouldn't set me up. Would they? On this trip I've met a lot of skeptical Irish horsemen who feel that some of my work is less than believable."

While I spoke, I scanned the audience, and it was easy to see that many people there were young, healthy and, by the look of them, probably competent horsemen. I went on to play a game with them.

"So I would like to have a volunteer," I said. "There are undoubtedly some very good horsemen here, who are younger and stronger than I am. I'll stand outside the pen and give advice if a volunteer will go in there and deal with this horse."

You could have heard a pin drop. The backside of every pair of trousers in the building was welded to a seat.

"Ahh," I said, "doesn't look like I'm going to get any volunteers. Guess I'll just have to do this one myself."

Join-up in its true form was out of the question. I had to get control of the situation before I could persuade this horse to trust me. I dug to the bottom of my bag and came out with a nylon lariat rope, the kind with which I had won a National Championship in Team Roping so many years before. I opened the gate once more and asked my rider to close it behind me. The instant I was in the pen I began to swing the rope around my head. Horses are inherently frightened of anything unfamiliar. Generally, flight animals will flee from something they don't understand. I hoped to create an image that Stanley had never seen before, and cause him to stay away from me for a few seconds.

I walked to the middle of the pen and watched Stanley closely as he tried to size me up. He seemed unable to come to grips with this strange sight and began to circle me, walking with his neck arched high. At the appropriate moment, I cast a loop that found its way around his neck just behind his jaws. As I drew it down, Stanley went into a bucking rage. He squalled and groaned, sounding more like a grizzly bear than a horse. Now he had a new concern. I was not the problem, the rope was. I gave him a little tug now and then, and he'd go into a renewed orbit, expressing all the rage he had inside him.

If there were six hundred people in that building, I had twelve hundred eyes locked on Stanley and me, and not even one was blinking. After about thirty or forty seconds, Stanley came to a stop. I moved in immediately, fashioning the rope into a come-along, the kind of halter I had used for many years to control difficult horses. The instant my rope was in place, Stanley began to cooperate. He went quiet and I didn't waste any time getting a saddle and bridle on him.

I rigged Stanley up on the long lines, even more quickly than I would normally do with a nonaggressive horse, and once he was on the lines I put him to work. I long-lined him for almost ten minutes instead of the normal two or three. In order to prepare him for my rider, I knew I had to do a fair bit of work. Excess energy with this big guy could prove to be lethal. At the appropriate moment, I brought in my rider, who happened to be an Irish racing exercise rider, Dermot O'Sullivan. He was a game lad to get on this incredible creature with the power of two ordinary horses. As I put him up, he said he thought the safest place to be in that round pen was actually on top of Stanley.

With a rider in the saddle, Stanley went to work in an orderly fashion. Once more, I gave him far more work to do than I would give a normal horse. He took it well and we finished the evening with our audience

Stanley as a mature stallion

amazed and full of questions. They surrounded me as soon as I left the round pen, and it was probably after midnight before Hugh and Fenton Flannely could pull me away. We went to Fenton's house for a drink and more conversation than I was up to at that late hour and after such a challenging evening.

Fenton confessed that Stanley had been vicious at the Dublin Horse Show a year before. He'd injured two people and been put in a dark box stall. Nobody had handled him since then, until that night. Ronnie McComb spoke up and said what they had just witnessed was unbelievable. Stanley was one of the most vicious horses anyone had ever known. Ronnie went on to tell me that the horse had set out to kill somebody on several different occasions in the past twelve months. I wanted to ask what the heck they were thinking, putting me in there without telling me these things, but somehow I knew they wouldn't have an acceptable answer anyway, so I didn't bother.

Five years later, in 1995, I returned to Fenton Flannely's place to give another demonstration. After the intermission, I was surprised to see that some fences had been placed in the arena, but I really didn't think much of it until Hugh McCusker and the rest of the team unveiled their surprise. Over the public address system a voice said, "Monty, this is Stanley. He is now Ireland's finest show-jumping Irish draft horse."

Stanley came into the ring groomed as if he was at a championship show, his mane braided. His rider took him in a large circle to give the audience a chance to appreciate how beautiful he was. She guided Stanley toward the first fence. Over he popped like a Thomson's gazelle, and he proceeded to jump each of the fences they had set for him. He stopped in the middle of the arena and his rider bowed slightly to the crowd. Then the announcer read what he said was a message from Stanley.

"Thank you for saving my life. They were about to send me on a one-way trip when I met you, Mr. Roberts, and I couldn't have blamed them for doing it. I was a very bad boy and I hated people, but you took the time to show me that it was OK to trust again. I am a champion now and I have you to thank for that."

I just stood there with tears running down my cheeks.

PRINCE OF DARKNESS

One day the phone rang and it was Sir Mark Prescott, a trainer in Newmarket, England. He said he had a horse called Prince of Darkness, owned by a partnership including both English and Americans. This was a horse with talent, but he had an absolute phobia about the starting gate.

By now I was leasing a facility in England: Bernice Cuthbert's Aston Park Stud. I wanted a base so remedial horses could be sent to me and I wouldn't have to travel as much, which would enable me to spend more time actually working on their problems. Sir Mark made arrangements to send Prince of Darkness to Aston Park Stud.

By any standards Prince of Darkness was huge; he stood about 17 hands and had a body with far more muscling than you normally see on a potential racehorse. He had a reputation for being a tough guy, and there were many stories about his years growing up on a farm in Ireland.

"He killed a steer when he was a yearling," his groom warned me. She also told me that the Prince had become extremely dangerous when anywhere near the starting gate.

I worked with him for about four days. After join-up, I schooled him in a training halter, and before long I had him approaching the starting gate. He was far more cooperative than his reputation had led me to believe he'd be. Although he seemed a bit disturbed by the gate, he would enter, stand quietly and leave it. I sent him back to Newmarket thinking he'd been one of the easiest starting-gate-phobic horses I had ever dealt with.

A week or so later I was back in California when a call came through. I immediately recognized Sir Mark's voice.

"Do you stand behind your work?" he asked.

"Sure I do. What's the problem?" I replied.

"This horse is not fixed and I need you here immediately, because I have some impatient owners who want results as soon as possible."

I was in Newmarket within a few days. Sir Mark, the groom and the exercise rider sat down with me to review every experience the Prince had had. It seemed that the enormous two-year-old had been fine with the gates during his first couple of training sessions. During the third session, the Prince had hesitated before fully entering the gate, and somebody had tapped him on his thigh. The Prince kicked back, hitting the rear portion of the apparatus, and from that point on, he hated the sight of the heap of metal, becoming a danger to both his handlers and himself.

I stayed with Sir Mark at Heath House, and it took the next three days to bring Prince of Darkness to the same point I had achieved on my earlier trip. This time, however, he was never relaxed in the gate and was inclined to kick frequently. He would even bite me as I worked near his head. Something was very wrong with the environment here in Newmarket, compared with Aston Park's. I explained my dilemma to Sir Mark and told him I suspected that the foot rails along the sides of the official gates were much larger than in the gates I had originally used. If simple claustrophobia was the culprit, it might be helpful to order up a horse van with adjustable partitions so I could squeeze Prince of Darkness into a very narrow space. This would allow me to test him while he was being driven, to see what his response might be. Sir Mark agreed and we scheduled the horse van for the following morning.

Sir Mark and I had dinner and a couple of glasses of wine, while I suppose I droned on about being frustrated to the tenth power. I told him that I was one sore, beat-up fifty-five-year-old cowboy. The Prince had bitten me several times, bashed me into the walls of the starting gate and run square over top of me on two different occasions.

"I'm at my wits' end," I said. I didn't understand how I could get him fixed and then have him go back to square one. It crossed my mind several times that I should return the payment I'd received and walk away from the seemingly impossible challenge.

We went to bed about ten o'clock, which was one hour late for Sir Mark. I made every attempt to get a good night's rest but sleep refused to come. I kept seeing playbacks of my work in my mind. I'd start to doze off and then one silly idea or another would hit me and I would be wide awake trying to make sense of plan after plan as they passed through my seemingly incompetent brain.

At around two in the morning I found myself pacing up and down the hall outside my bedroom. Soft footsteps sounded and a door opened to reveal Sir Mark looking at me quizzically. Wrapped in a bathrobe, he stood in his doorway, silently questioning why I was walking up and down, disturbing his sleep, too.

"I'm sorry if I disturbed you, but I can't sleep. I can't seem to get my brain to stop working."

Sir Mark came and stood near the window, his face cast in moonlight. Suddenly his expression sharpened.

"Well, I'll be," he muttered softly. "Come and see this."

I looked out the window to the stable yard below. In the moonlight we could see Prince of Darkness pacing back and forth in his stall. He too was wide awake.

"That's three of us trying to work out what the heck is wrong," said Sir Mark.

Then he told me how the horse had been named. He'd killed that steer in his paddock in Ireland and played with it like a cat with a mouse. Sir Mark said the starting gates were just not built for a horse his size. When the Prince was in the starting gate, his nose touched the front gate while his hindquarters were crowded by the rear one. Sir Mark said he could see the foot rails pressing into his sides even when the Prince was standing quietly.

"Now I'm going to leave the two of you to execute your gentle battle of wills," he said. Sir Mark needed to be in the stable by five and he had to get some sleep. "You two work on your problems as quietly as you can, and if you have to give up, I'll notify the owners. While I don't know if they'll understand, I certainly will."

The horse van arrived about seven o'clock the following morning, and I conducted a series of tests. I found that I could squeeze the Prince as tightly as I wanted while the driver negotiated sharp turns all around

Newmarket. The lack of negative response from the Prince proved he didn't mind being hemmed in—claustrophobia was not his problem. We returned to Heath House and I reported my findings to Sir Mark. I was happy that I had at least discovered something about our puzzle.

A training gate I had designed was in place at the training stable Warren Hill. It had been built so that the foot rails could be removed, and I began to work with the Prince with no rails at all. Lo and behold, he was the perfect student. I replaced the rails and put the Prince back in the gate. I stood in front of him and moved him slightly forward and back, as I often do to test a horse's acceptance of the gate. He exploded, knocking me down and running right over top of me. I had a thirty-foot line on him so he didn't get loose, but I was nearly unconscious as I staggered up with the Prince at the end of the line. The groom and a friend of Sir Mark's, Geraldine Rees, the first woman to complete the Grand National, both ran over to me. Geraldine pointed out that I was bleeding from a laceration by my left ear.

"It's the rails," I exclaimed. "We need to remove the rails and everything will be OK."

Geraldine gave me a ride down the hill to Heath House where I washed my ear and stuck a bandage on it while Sir Mark phoned a racing steward he knew to find out whether rails could be removed from the starting gate. Unfortunately it was against the rules to change the starting gate in any way. We would just have to figure out how to live with the rails.

I told Sir Mark that I believed the Prince felt as though the rails were biting him. When he kicked out, the rails caused more pain, reinforcing that idea. His intuitive reaction came from his ancestors' experiences with attacking wolves or packs of dogs.

Geraldine drove me back to Warren Hill and I took up where I'd left off. The training gate allowed me to school the Prince with no rails, very small rails and medium rails, as well as with regulation-size rails. He could handle the tiny ones, but that was it. With anything larger, he'd become a demon. I was in a sorry state of discouragement when I began muttering to Geraldine about an idea that was passing through my head.

"You know those leather pads that protect the picador's horse in Spanish bullfights?" I asked. Geraldine knew exactly what I was referring to. I went on to say that if I could cover the Prince's hips with a very heavy leather blanket, he might not feel the rails. The trip in the horse-box had shown he was fine with smooth walls. The heavy leather blanket could be pulled off as he ran out of the stalls.

"It's all a dream, anyway," I said, "because even if I could make such a contraption, it would take a huge amount of leather and weigh a ton. How would you ever get it on the horse at the races?"

Geraldine looked at me and uttered the words that would change the course of racing from that point on.

"What about using carpet?" she said.

The light went on. Carpet was the answer.

We drove to a carpet store in Newmarket, bought some remnant pieces and hurried to Gibson Saddlers, where I began to design the kind of covering I felt might work. To create a prototype, I asked that bits of carpet be sewn to the inside and the outside of a regular stable blanket. It would be shaped in such a way that it would protect the hips and flanks of the horse. The Gibson people were very cooperative, and I was back at the stable within two hours to try it out. The moment I put the blanket on Prince of Darkness, I could sense a feeling of relaxation come over him.

As we began to work through the starting gate, it was obvious we had finally met his needs. I gave Geraldine a pat on the back and congratulated her for coming up with the carpet idea. We had saved this horse's career. I worked him in and out several times and was convinced we had solved the problem.

Realizing that the following day was Good Friday and shops would be closed for business, we raced back to Gibson's to modify the blanket so that it could be used at the races. With the addition of a breast collar and a ring at the back with which to pull it off when the race began, we had our design. Prince of Darkness was scheduled to race on the Monday and we had precious little time to prepare.

Sir Mark had to go to France on Friday, but he telephoned the racing stewards at Warwick racecourse and prevailed upon them to approve the use of the carpet. George Duffield would be the jockey, and he would drive me to the races with my carpet tucked away in the trunk of the car. When I met George, he seemed game to try the invention but a little embarrassed.

"Carpet? He's wearing a carpet?"

"That's what it's made of, sure."

"Is it patterned carpet, or plain?"

"It has a slight pattern, I suppose you'd say."

"Oh no," he groaned.

"Don't you like patterned carpet?"

George held his hands up in mock surrender.

"No . . . it's fine. I don't mind looking like an idiot. Maybe I ought to wear the same pattern. Let's go for it. Trade in the silks. Can we stop at a carpet shop on the way and measure me up for a tufted Wilton?"

I assured him that Prince of Darkness had to have his magic carpet or he'd refuse to start.

At Warwick, the head starter was similarly apprehensive about the blanket, but Sir Mark had been given permission to use the unconventional apparatus, and the stewards couldn't back out now.

When I put the blanket up behind George, we heard a lot of comments from the other jockeys. I remember Willy Carson laughing and asking George if he planned to wear it throughout the running.

"Sure," George replied. "None of your horses will pass me if I make the lead wearing this thing."

Prince of Darkness entered the gate without fuss and stood totally relaxed. When the starter pushed the button, he flew the fastest of the eighteen horses, leaving the blanket behind as planned. Success!

As the horses were running, I felt an arm around my shoulders and turned to see the smiling face of Geraldine Rees—I'd had no idea she'd made the trip. We were one pair of happy horsemen at that moment.

Prince of Darkness went on to be a good winner, and though he was never a champion, he paved the way for thousands of horses to experience successful racing careers after balking at the first test, the starting gate. Apparently, more than ten thousand horses have used the blanket since 1990.

THE OSBALDESTON
HORSE

One of the cities I was scheduled to visit on a 1995 tour of England was a place called Osbaldeston, in the north. I would be appearing at a large equestrian center there to address a number of horse issues, one of which was the problem of transport. Horses are often treated in a very brutal way when they refuse to load, and it's not necessary. I've proved this countless times.

I arrived at the center at midday and was soon approached by a girl of about twelve years of age. She had brought a horse that was impossible to load in a trailer. I asked if she was sure it was impossible, and she told me she was absolutely certain. I suppose I was being facetious when I inquired, "So, if he's impossible to load in a trailer, how did you get here?"

"I rode him," she said. "I rode twenty-five miles yesterday and five miles this morning. I stayed with some friends last night and got here about an hour ago."

I was stunned. When I asked this brave little girl if she'd made the trip all by herself, she told me her mother had come along in the car and checked on her from time to time, but often she rode on her own. She told me she could win with her horse in shows but she had to ride to the competitions. She explained that her father traveled a lot with his work, mostly away from England, and when he'd discovered she'd ridden for three days, staying with friends, in order to get to one competition, he was very upset. Now her horse would be destroyed if I couldn't solve the problem.

I was frozen as I contemplated the gravity of the situation. Her father couldn't have known what it was like for a twelve-year-old girl to have a wonderful horse in her life and be faced with such a dilemma. But he had every right to be concerned about her riding on the roads. I felt confident that I could fix her problem, and I would show her how to load the horse herself and satisfy her dad.

Schooling a horse to back up comfortably while being handled from the ground is critical to my system of dealing with a difficult loader, and I asked her if her horse backed up well. She assured me that it was extremely easy to back him. I didn't go to see her horse because I never touch any of the horses I use in demonstrations until the audience is present, and I had decided to take this one for my loading demonstration. He would be the final horse of the event.

It was about ten o'clock when the bay gelding was led to the center of my round pen. The girl took the microphone and told the audience her story. There was total silence as she described the difficulties she and her family had faced for the last three years or so. I did a join-up with the horse, which seemed to go quite well. He was following me around the pen within four or five minutes.

With my training halter in place, I began the schooling process designed to get the horse to lead forward easily, stop on cue and back up without hesitation. But when I got to the backing-up part, it was as though he'd grown roots in the ground. I couldn't back him one step, no matter what I did. The girl was sitting on a chair near the gate where the horse had entered the ring. Speaking into the microphone so that everyone could hear, I looked at her and said, "This afternoon you told me your horse backed really well. Now that I'm out here trying it, I find it's next to impossible. Why did you tell me he would back up easily?"

"If you want him to back up, Mr. Roberts, take him over by that trailer and see how he backs up then," she replied. With that, the audience roared with laughter.

It was at this point that I first became fully aware of the phenomenon of a horse using reverse to gain the upper hand. Since then the primary theme of my loading demonstrations has been cooperative backing. When the horse owns reverse gear for himself, he can use reverse against you whenever he chooses. Reverse must be owned by a partnership of man and horse and should be a direction that is executed by both members of the partnership. Cooperative backing is extremely important in the training of a horse.

When the laughter subsided and I, too, had composed myself, I continued to work with my training halter to get a step or two in reverse. After about six or seven minutes, I was achieving good cooperation. Once I could walk with the horse willingly following, stop and have the horse halt at my shoulder, and then back comfortably as part of the routine, it was time to approach the trailer. I led the gelding toward it, stopping and backing up periodically as we came closer to the vehicle. I suppose the horse and I looked like we were performing a kind of dance. When I felt a good level of willingness on the part of my equine student, I asked him to enter the trailer.

The horse followed me straight in. As I came out, I could see that the girl was in a state of shock. She was sitting with her mouth open, and when I asked her to take the mike and respond to us, she was speechless. I loaded the horse ten or twelve times and ended the evening with the girl loading him herself. She beamed with pride as she walked her horse in and out of the trailer several times. She stopped at one point and threw her arms around his neck, with tears rolling down each cheek. She thanked me with a big hug, too.

She told me that some friends had brought a trailer with them, and I later met them with the girl and her mother. The child loaded her horse probably fifteen times before they drove off into the darkness, waving goodbye.

Since meeting that horse ten years ago, I have conducted demonstrations all over the world and have told the story of him and his owner at every one of them. Loading problems have become for many attendees the cornerstone of my events. The Osbaldeston horse was responsible for giving me a level of understanding that has since allowed me to do approximately 1,500 non-loaders without failure.

LOMITAS AND
THE GERMAN DYNASTY

In 1988, a German-bred mare by the name of La Colorada by Surumu gave birth to a copper chestnut colt named Lomitas. At nineteen months of age, he was placed with a Bremen racing trainer, Andreas Wohler, who knew very early on that he had a talented baby on his hands. He was careful to limit the horse's training as a two-year-old, and Lomitas had only two starts in 1990, winning both. Because they were important two-year-old races, Lomitas was named the champion in that category for the 1990 season.

The horse was owned by Walther Jacobs, founder of Gestüt Fährhof of Bremen, one of Germany's leading breeding and racing establishments. Early in 1991, excitement was palpable among the Jacobs family and at the Wohler stable. They had the early favorite for the German Derby in July, and it appeared that he was by far the best of his age group. While Andreas knew that Lomitas was a bit of a handful at times, he was confident that there'd be no problem racing him in April. That confidence was shattered when Lomitas refused to enter the starting gate. A full starting crew battled with him for a very dangerous twenty minutes and eventually got him in. He went on to win the race easily.

Disappointed but not panicked, everyone in the organization went to work to prepare Lomitas for a test in front of the stewards, which was required because of his behavior at the starting gate. Although he passed the test, his performance was pretty dodgy. It took five to seven minutes to get him into the gate and he was very nervous while in there. Nonetheless, he was cleared to travel to Cologne in May for his second race as a three-year-old. By then, all derby prospects should have completed their preparatory races and been fit to perform at the highest level the first week of July.

Lomitas didn't want to load into the horse van to travel to Cologne, and it took us two hours to get him in. When it came time to enter the starting gate, he simply refused. Considering the importance of the owner and the young horse, the racetrack crew did their best to get him into the gate. They blindfolded Lomitas, yanked his tail over his back—the jockey actually held it over his shoulder—and pushed and pulled. The men literally wrestled with him for about thirty minutes, until he became violent and attacked them, kicking and striking out with his feet. The stewards radioed to disqualify him. Lomitas lay on the ground, totally exhausted from the battle and in disgrace, as the race started without him.

This catastrophic incident resulted in the immediate banning of Lomitas from racing worldwide. The embarrassment for the family was overwhelming, and for Andreas Wohler, the incident was a trainer's worst nightmare.

As Mr. Jacobs was leaving the racetrack, the trainer John Gosden went over to speak to him. He was very upset because a horse he'd transported from England for this race had been injured while waiting in the starting gate for Lomitas to load. Mr. Jacobs could only apologize.

"You need Monty Roberts," John Gosden said, and somehow Mr. Jacobs remembered my name. He called Andreas Wohler the next day and asked that he contact me. On June 12, 1991, I put my life on hold and left for Germany.

At the Bremen airport I noticed a young man in riding breeches waiting around and thought he might be a lad sent to meet me.

"Do you know Andreas Wohler?" I asked.

"I'm Andreas Wohler," he said.

We drove straight to the Bremen racecourse, where Andreas operated a training stable for up to a hundred Thoroughbreds. What happened next takes its place alongside my memories of Ginger and Brownie, my marriage to Pat, the birth of our children, my days with Johnny Tivio and my first meeting with Queen Elizabeth. There'd be a time before Lomitas and a time after him.

When I first saw the magnificent horse, the single word "Gorgeous!" flew from my mouth. The chestnut Thoroughbred stallion stood 16 hands and weighed about 1,150 pounds. He had a white pastern on the off hind

*A terrible time in his life: Lomitas is disqualified from racing,
Cologne, Germany, May 1991.*

leg and a star between his eyes with an elongated strip that widened and
ended between his nostrils. Every point of his skeletal frame hit its mark,
creating the near-perfect racehorse conformation.

I walked over to where he was munching hay and stood against the back
of his stall to greet him with a stroke on his neck. "Hello, Lomitas, you're a
fine man, eh?"

I moved my hands back along his body and felt him wanting to push
into my hands, away from the wall. I held out against the pressure and he
immediately kicked out. I logged this behavior as a possible response to
any number of things and continued making his acquaintance. He was a
breathtaking animal with a look in his eye that spoke of high intelligence.
I had traveled a long way to be standing here and suddenly I felt very
pleased to have made the journey. My task was specific: cure this horse of
his starting-gate phobia.

As I'd requested, Andreas had constructed a solid-wall permanent train-ing stall, which was much safer than the conventional kind. I had also asked for an assistant who could speak English and knew horses well. Obviously, if I was to train someone to work with Lomitas in my absence, he would also have to speak German. Andreas introduced me to a young man by the name of Simon Stokes. Simon, originally from England, was a steeplechase jockey who at this point was considering retiring from jump racing. He seemed to have everything I needed. He was bilingual and had plenty of experience. Although I didn't know it at the time, Simon would prove to be a champion equal to Lomitas himself, and Pat and I would come to think of him and his wife, Cordula, and daughter, Celine, as immediate family.

On the first day, I took Lomitas to a small covered exercise track, not much bigger than a hallway. I led him into the structure and backed him up to a point near the end of the lead rope. I asked him to step toward me. He seemed very reluctant to cooperate. I raised one arm sharply above my head and then the other. He didn't seem unduly alarmed, which told me that he probably hadn't been abused with whips.

The reason I tested Lomitas for signs of abuse wasn't that I distrusted Andreas or Simon. It was because I always accord my horses the respect of asking them to speak for themselves. I've been lied to by people but never by a horse. Lying just isn't in their makeup. And while most people do try to give me the straight story, it's sometimes quite different from the horse's version.

I could see that Lomitas had a good relationship with humans and began to think his problem might be claustrophobia. I led him back to a spot near his stable and was walking him in circles when Andreas and Simon returned. I gave them a short report on my get-acquainted session and asked Andreas if there was a round pen or lunging ring nearby. I told him that I needed to turn Lomitas loose in order to gain his trust. Andreas had never heard of join-up and didn't know anything about my training meth-ods. He knew of a show-jumping ring about ten miles away, but he thought that transporting Lomitas there would probably be out of the question.

"If he doesn't want to go on the truck," I said, "that will be part of our training program."

Both Andreas and Simon were nervous about loading Lomitas but agreed to telephone the transport company. We soon had a beautiful horse van at our disposal, and Andreas suggested backing it into the barn with the ramp in the center aisle. He said they'd done this before and used horse blankets to frighten Lomitas onto the truck.

"He's going to have to learn to load like a gentleman if I'm to work with him," I said. "I'll school him with my training halter, and then we'll ask him to load."

Lomitas turned out to be a very good student and quickly learned to respect both the halter and me. I decided that I would treat him like a regular horse until he caused me a problem. I started to load him into the van, walking up the ramp, and Lomitas followed me. The instant he was inside, the helpers ran to lift the ramp.

"No," I told them. "Leave the ramp down. I'm going to walk him off and on several times."

A wonderful time in his life: Lomitas wins in Germany, June 1991.

Some Irish exercise riders working nearby called out, "If you bring him off, you'll never get him back on again."

I asked them to have a little faith. With disbelief they watched as I walked Lomitas off and on the van about fifteen to twenty times without incident. We closed up the ramp and drove away.

I rode in the back of the truck to watch how the young horse would react to adrenaline-raising situations, just as I had done with Prince of Darkness. He seemed fine and we made the trip to the show-jumping yard without any trouble. When the van came to a stop, I again led Lomitas off and on several times.

Andreas, Simon and I used jump poles to set up a sort of round pen approximately fifty feet in diameter in one corner of the arena. I released Lomitas and allowed him to canter away from me. Within a minute or two, he was giving me all the signals I look for before asking a horse to join up with me. Within another few minutes, we were in full conversation. Now I wanted to take his trust a bit further. We dismantled our make-believe round pen and gave Lomitas the run of the arena. He immediately moved away from me and seemed to want to take charge, to dictate what our relationship should be. After about five minutes, I was able to persuade him to see me as a partner rather than an adversary. He started to follow me wherever I went.

I showed Andreas and Simon my technique for gaining the trust of a horse, and after less than an hour, we were ready to load up again for the return trip. Andreas and Simon were prepared for trouble, but Lomitas remained calm and walked into the horse van without hesitation. I had overcome several obstacles with him and felt good about our chances of success. I slept well that night.

The next day I began to work with Lomitas at the permanent training gate. Banking on the trust I had already created, I soon had him going in and out of it without problems. When Simon finished with his regular duties, I asked him to put some tack on Lomitas and sit on him as I continued to lead him in and out of the gate. By the time we finished the training session, Lomitas was letting me close the gate behind him, and he was walking out the front in a very relaxed manner. We'd managed to bridge another gap on our way to solving his starting-gate phobia.

That afternoon the head starter from the Bremen racecourse, Mr. Dunker, dropped by to check on Lomitas's progress. Even though he spoke very little English, I could tell he was skeptical about Lomitas. Still, he agreed to recommend that the horse be tested to assess the possibility of lifting his ban.

The following morning, June 16, a group of five racing officials gathered on the Bremen racecourse as I brought Lomitas to a set of regulation gates placed on the turf near the official racing surface. Terry Hellier, the primary jockey for Andreas Wohler at the time, was up. I must say he was a brave and calm young man.

Lomitas entered the gate, stood relatively quietly and broke acceptably. The stewards were impressed but quick to point out that I had worked with him for only a couple of days. They wanted to test Lomitas one more time, with horses on either side of him, before the ban would be lifted. The test was set for June 18 and Andreas targeted a race for June 23.

I continued to school Lomitas and he passed his test with flying colors. The stewards cautiously reinstated him for one race. They asked that I bring Lomitas to the start myself—no racetrack employees were to handle him. This suited me just fine.

I felt tense on the morning of the race. Nearly twenty thousand fans were at the racecourse, and they all seemed to be watching Lomitas and me as we walked toward the starting gate. The horse had become something of a folk hero for German racing fans. Parents held their children over the rail as they called out, "Lomie, Lomie, Lomie."

The stewards had decided that I would be last to load my horse and that I would have ten minutes, maximum, to get the job done. But as I walked Lomitas in circles behind the gate, I realized something was wrong. All of the other jockeys and horses were gathered on the far side of the track. The trainers were there, too, and they appeared to be having some sort of meeting. Andreas came over to me and said, "They want to boycott the race unless Lomitas goes in first. They want to see that he's OK before they enter."

"Let's go," I said. "I'll go in first."

"Are you crazy?" Andreas said. "We have permission to go in last, and it'll be much harder to load him with no horses in there."

I turned and walked straight into my assigned gate with Lomitas quietly accompanying me. The head starter shouted to the rest of the jockeys and they immediately began to load their horses. Ironically, track officials had a number of problems with some of them. When we were finally all in, Lomitas broke well with the field. He stayed in third spot for most of the race and then sped away from the field in the last quarter of a mile. It was an incredible pleasure to see him take his rightful place in the winner's circle.

This triumph would only be the first of a series of victories for Lomitas. Later that year, he was named Germany's champion three-year-old and Horse of the Year. I traveled to Germany often throughout 1991 to assist in Lomitas's races, but Simon Stokes also became very adept at handling him. He was eventually offered the job of racing manager for Gestüt Fährhof, a position he has held for over ten years.

Lomitas after retirement

Lomitas went on to amass a record that, in my opinion, is more important than that of any other racehorse I've dealt with. He wasn't the biggest money-earner, but with three Group I races to his credit and Horse of the Year honors, he surpasses even Alleged as my favorite racehorse of all time. Lomitas won a total of ten races and had three seconds and one third, collecting $918,656. I seldom use the word "great" to describe an individual, but I attach it to Lomitas with confidence. It's unlikely I'll ever work with another horse that will achieve so much. Still, the most satisfying aspect about my experience with him was the close emotional attachment we formed. Knowing him is a privilege I'll cherish for the rest of my days.

After my success with Lomitas, Walther Jacobs asked me to become a consultant to his operation and to see to the starting of each of his babies before their training at the racing stables. I was pleased to take on both of these roles.

The first group of American yearlings I sent to Fährhof included Quebrada, by Devil's Bag out of Queen to Conquer. The second group included Risen Raven, by Risen Star out of Aurania, and then came Macanal, by Northern Flagship out of Magnala. These three all became champions and high earners. Simon and I have started over three hundred young Thoroughbreds for Fährhof. Of these, six went on to become classic winners, thirty-nine were Group winners (in internationally approved Group stakes races) with fifty-six listed winners (in internationally approved stakes races). Lavirco and Suraco, both foaled in 1993, finished first and second in the 1996 German Derby and Suraco went on to win $1,020,000.

Another of my early tasks for Walther Jacobs was to buy a group of broodmares for Lomitas. His second career at stud proved to be even more important than his first as a racehorse. When I found Spirit of Eagles, I wrote on her pedigree the word "sprinter," because she ran most of her races at six furlongs. I liked her conformation and the fact that she was very sound, with fifty-nine starts in her racing career. In 1996, when bred to Lomitas, she produced Silvano. He won his only start as a two-year-old.

CLOCKWISE FROM TOP *Macanal, Lavirco and Risen Raven*

The following year he raced five times, winning twice, including a Group II race. At four years of age, he raced four times, each one a Group race, and was in the money every time.

In 2001, Silvano really hit his stride. He won the Group I Singapore Cup, breaking a track record. He also won the Group I Arlington Million in Chicago and the Group II Queen Elizabeth II Cup as well as coming second in the Group I Man o' War Stakes in New York. He was named Germany's Horse of the Year and, with career earnings of $2,321,024, was retired to stud in 2002 with an international rating of 121, which places him in the top one half of 1 percent of the world's racehorses. Lomitas also

OPPOSITE *Spirit of Eagles*
BELOW *Silvano at the Sha Tin racecourse for the Hong Kong Invitational (Queen Elizabeth II Cup) in 2001. The jockey is Andreas Suborics.*

Sabiango

produced the winner of the 1999 Group I German Derby: the champion three-year-old and Horse of the Year Belenus. I encouraged Sheikh Mohammed bin Rashid al Maktoum of Dubai, the world's leading owner, to buy breeding rights to Lomitas, and he responded by buying seven lifetime spots. Lomitas is now a champion sire standing in Newmarket to a full book of ninety mares. Because of Sheikh Mohammed's influence, seven of the mares are from the world's leading broodmare band. To date, Lomitas's offspring have won nearly $8 million.

Sabiango, a foal of 1999, is another son of Spirit of Eagles, this time by Acatenango, who stands at stud at Gestüt Fährhof. A major Group I winner, Sabiango is still racing. Spirit of Eagles was named broodmare of the world for 2001. That same year, Fährhof purchased a yearling at auction, a chestnut filly called Royal Dubai, by Dashing Blade out of Reem Dubai. In 2002 she became the eighth champion produced by Fährhof since I joined it in 1991.

Walther Jacobs's grandson, Dr. Andreas Jacobs, is now chairman of the board. He issued the following statement:

The year 2001 has been the most significant in the racing history of Gestüt Fährhof. Our breeding and racing program has attained new heights on a broader international scale than I could have dreamed possible. Victory in the Arlington Million has rewritten the record books of Gestüt Fährhof. Monty Roberts saved the racing career of Lomitas and then brought us Spirit of Eagles and several other fine young mares. Monty started Silvano and Sabiango as well as virtually all of the youngsters Fährhof has produced. Fährhof is the result of a team effort and right from foaling time there are many people who give their energy to the production of fine racehorses. Simon Stokes, our racing manager, and Andreas Wohler, the trainer of both Silvano and Sabiango, should also be mentioned as contributing greatly to the success of our program.

I thank the Jacobs family for their confidence. Gestüt Fährhof has been a dream come true for me. My association with the operation has allowed me to use my life's experiences with some of the best breeding in Europe. It's so much fun for me to spend about a month each year working with wonderful young Thoroughbreds and doing it from daylight to dark. The opportunity to work alongside Simon Stokes has afforded me the chance to pass on the knowledge I have gathered from the tens of thousands of horses I have dealt with over the past decades. To think I learned from American mustangs that can be bought for $125 and now work with virtually every breed. Each day of my life I am grateful for the chances I have had to experience horses across the broadest base of disciplines. I hope the concepts I've discovered will be carried forward to create a deeper understanding between man and horse.

DAYFLOWER,
LA CONFÉDÉRATION
and SONG OF AFRICA

After my experiences with Prince of Darkness and Lomitas, the international horse network zeroed in on me as someone who could mend problem horses. We were receiving four or five calls a week from all over the world and I had to pick and choose which cases to take on. There were simply not enough squares on the calendar to deal with all of them.

One day I got a call from Henry Cecil. He had a filly in training at Warren Hill with a serious aversion to the starting gate. She belonged to Sheikh Mohammed, a serious and accomplished horseman who owns more Thoroughbreds than anyone else in the world. This filly, called Dayflower, was one of his favorites, and he wanted me to work with her as a special favor.

I remember as if it were yesterday the day I stood in the middle of Henry Cecil's large walking circle behind the stables and watched as Dayflower approached from the north end, led by an assistant named Steven Dible with Henry walking behind. I believe I must have felt a lot like Prince Rainier of Monaco when he first laid eyes on Grace Kelly, spellbound by the beauty and regal bearing of the gorgeous creature.

"How is she bred?" I asked Henry, and he told me that she was by Majestic Light out of Equate by Raja Baba.

Dayflower walked in a most effortless way and seemed to be totally at

A winning day for Dayflower in England

ease with her surroundings. Steven, better known by his nickname, Yarmie, stopped her, and she looked over at me with two of the most beautiful eyes I have ever seen on a horse—large, black and doelike.

Henry told me they had managed to get her in my solid wooden training gate a few times but never in regulation metal gates—they were certain death as far as she was concerned. He told me he had never before seen a horse so frightened of the starting gate, and Henry had seen a lot of horses in his time.

I asked Yarmie to lead Dayflower around the stable to an area where we could see the regulation gate. He said he'd have to stay about a hundred yards away from it because she'd become so phobic.

When we rounded the end of the row of stables and came into view of the gate, Dayflower stopped in her tracks. With her ears up and eyes intently fixed on the gate, she began to quiver as if the temperature had dropped below freezing. Soon her whole body was in a state of spasm, and her skin bounced up and down as if she were standing on a vibrator. It was then that I saw something I had never seen before and have never seen since: huge droplets of perspiration were rising to the tips of her dry hair and rolling off. After two to three minutes, Dayflower was as wet as if she'd just taken a bath. The sight was shocking. This would be a daunting challenge, indeed.

I took her to the round pen, did my initial join-up work with her and schooled her in a training halter. I spent more than an hour that afternoon just trying to get her somewhere near the gate that frightened her so, and I began to sense that she was happier if the gate was up against a solid wall. With the wall on one side, she had less freedom to take flight in a way that was dangerous to her.

Over the next few days I worked with Dayflower for many hours and managed to convince her that the gate wouldn't kill her. Eventually, after a lot of reassuring, patting and congratulating, she could handle them with poise. We progressed to the racecourse starting gate and, because of the foundation we had laid, she was able to cope with it well after just two sessions.

I left Dayflower in the care of Henry Cecil's staff. Yarmie had worked with me on several remedial horses before and was able to continue my work after I left. Dayflower remained one of Sheikh Mohammed's favorites, and although she never won any classic races, she did win four times, earning a total of $81,048.

At the time, I didn't realize how significant an impact Dayflower had made on me. But because she had requested a solid wall to help her overcome her extreme fear of the gate, she helped me help literally thousands of other horses with a similar phobia. A dark bay filly called La Confédération and another mare, Song of Africa, would extend that lesson.

When I first heard about La Confédération, the story I was told made my blood run cold. Anthony Stroud called me on behalf of Sheikh Mohammed, the owner, and told me the only way they could get La Confédération into her box stall was to put a pungent substance in her nose to take away her ability to smell, blindfold her and, at a fair distance from the stable, spin her in circles so as to disorient her. Approaching the stall, several lads would assist the groom by locking arms behind her and bracing from each side, literally pushing her through the door.

I cleared my calendar and caught the first flight to Paris en route to Chantilly and the stables of one of Europe's leading Thoroughbred trainers, André Fabre. At Charles de Gaulle airport I was met by one of his exercise riders. Fluent in French even though his first language was English, the young man was wearing a cowboy hat. I called him Tex.

On the way to Chantilly, Tex told me he had been assigned to the project so he could learn the ropes, but in his opinion, nothing could be done for the filly. She had shown some talent in her speed tests but, according to Tex, God had put her brain in backward when he made her. Her problems had nothing to do with her environment or experiences; she was simply wired wrong. At the time, they had around two hundred horses in training and none of the others had problems like this filly's. Not only was it nearly impossible to get her into her box stall, but it was equally difficult to get her out. And as far as transportation was concerned, there was no way to load her short of using heavy tranquilizers and many men to push her. They had attempted the starting gate once, but it was such a frightening experience for her that the rider was thrown and she ran through the forest to get away from the apparatus.

Driving into Chantilly is an experience that any horseman would savor. It's the most beautiful training ground anywhere in the world. Hundreds of years old, the training tracks are carved out of forests that were standing before horses were domesticated. As Tex and I drove by the lake and the château, I remembered the story of the former ruler of the area. He'd left his tiny kingdom to the government of France with the proviso that it forever remain a training grounds for horses. It is said that he believed in reincarnation and wanted to come back as a racehorse to live in his beloved Chantilly. La Confédération was the eighth or tenth horse I had worked with there, and both Pat and I had come to love the place.

By the time we arrived at the training stables, I must admit I was having doubts about whether I could do anything for this deeply troubled filly. It was close to noon when I first saw her, and she seemed perfectly normal as she munched on some hay in a spacious stall that was part of a stone stable more than a hundred years old. Though not as beautiful as Dayflower, she was quite attractive, athletically speaking, and I could easily see why Sheikh Mohammed's team had advised her purchase.

André Fabre's yard is as beautiful as any I have ever seen. Six stone buildings house the horses, and each one could have won an architectural award at some time. Each building is set up with thirty to forty box stalls, and the surfaces in and around the buildings are works of art, with cobblestones laid in patterns. The walkways for the horses are about twelve feet wide with a deep cushion of shredded bark, creating a safe surface.

Escorting me to a spacious office, Tex introduced me to André Fabre, who was poring over charts of the day's workouts. He was obviously very busy, and our meeting was brief and to the point. André told me that Sheikh Mohammed had great confidence in my work and felt I could cure La Confédération of her phobias. However, he emphasized that he had never encountered such a troubled young Thoroughbred, and if I couldn't see a way to help her, I should let him know as soon as possible so he could tell the sheikh.

Tex then took me to a small café where many of the exercise riders were having lunch. It felt strange to be in the presence of so many people who were discussing horses and yet I could hardly understand a word of what they were saying. He told me that La Confédération was the topic of conversation throughout Chantilly. Virtually everyone had an opinion one way or another about whether I could solve her problems. Apparently, most of them thought I had no chance.

We were back at the yard by one thirty and I checked the equipment that had been ordered for me. The custom-made blanket that had been sent by Gibson Saddlers seemed to be just fine. I fit protective leg boots on La Confédération, who stood quite comfortably. Then I checked the special halters I had brought with me to be sure they were the right size.

My first goal was to convince La Confédération that she should walk quietly in and out of her box stall. She had obviously never been trained to back up well from the ground, and I must have worked for twenty minutes or so on that alone. I then put the special protective blanket on her. Within five minutes or so she seemed comfortable wearing it as I walked her, stopped her and backed her up, all within the confines of her stall. When she was able to back up with ease, I began to back her toward the door instead of trying to move through it in the conventional manner. "That's a girl, Connie," I told her, as she managed to get her hind legs onto the cobblestones just outside her stable.

We worked for about an hour, at the end of which I could back Connie out of the stall, continue to ask her to back up, negotiate a circle and back her into the stall. Tex was quite amazed. I asked him to take a turn to get a feel for the halter. Within an hour and a half, I was walking her forward in and out of her box stall, taking a few steps at a time.

Throughout the training session, Connie was sending me a signal: it seemed that she'd hit her hip on the wooden frame of the door at some point, and that's what had set up her phobia about the door. The pain she had felt had created a fear that spilled over to encompass the starting gate and transport vehicle as well. She seemed totally relaxed and comfortable now as she followed me. Her pulse rate was low and her adrenaline level was more than acceptable.

It must have been around five thirty when I decided that Connie had had enough. Tex set up her feed in her box stall and I led her inside. I removed her blanket as she reached for her grain tub and then stripped off her halter so she could dig right in. Her disposition stayed sweet as I removed the four protective leg boots. Her appetite was obviously keen, which was a good sign. Nervous tension can cause Thoroughbreds, particularly fillies, to back away from their food. Connie was eating up a storm, so I knew she wasn't traumatized by our long schooling session.

We left the stable and Tex showed me the horse van that would be our schoolroom the following morning. Equipped with state-of-the-art safety features, it was painted in the colors of André Fabre and had signs alerting drivers that it carried racing Thoroughbreds. I gave the truck a thorough inspection, and then we walked the short distance to the permanent training gate that had been constructed for me in a clearing among the beautiful old-growth trees. The design was the same as the one in Henry Cecil's yard, where I had schooled Prince of Darkness, Dayflower and many others. Nearby was a round pen about sixty feet in diameter. It looked as though it had been there for many decades and used as a lunging ring or turnout. Tex told me that the regulation training gates were about half a mile away in a forested area.

We drove to the Alibird Hotel, about three miles from the stable, where I would be staying, and Tex said he'd pick me up at six the next morning. I told him I'd need at least four and possibly six days to accomplish my goals. I don't know why I gave him that estimate; at the time I knew nothing of the depth of Connie's phobias. While I was confident that we could load her comfortably into the truck the following morning, the starting gate was haunting me.

Back at the stables early the next morning, we found that Connie had finished her breakfast and seemed to be feeling well. I gave her a little refresher course with the evil stall door, and she passed all her tests within fifteen to twenty minutes. Tex followed as I led Connie toward the horse van, and oh boy, was she upset when she caught sight of it!

The truck was placed on good footing, and Connie was wearing her boots, protective blanket and head protector in case she reared while inside. We put some wings—fencelike panels—on the ramp and a wall behind her, and finally she agreed to make the trip up and into the truck. The phobia was cracked. Connie would now load and unload with no problem. It was only around eight in the morning of my first full day, but I had already overcome many of my filly's psychological problems with nary a scratch. My confidence soared.

The exercise riders were in the habit of taking a breakfast break at eight thirty, so Tex and I took Connie back to her stall, stripped her down and decided to give her an hour to eat, drink and rest. We returned at nine thirty to suit her up for her next schooling session at the round pen. I did a successful join-up with her; Connie was highly communicative and intelligent, and within fifteen minutes she was happily following me wherever I went. Tex placed the protective blanket on Connie and she accepted it straight away, having already worn it in the stable. I schooled her with the training halter, moving her forward, back, left and right. She was fully cooperative as I led her from the ring toward the training gate. With complete assurance, I walked up behind the gate and asked her to enter the narrow structure. I believe it was during my second or third request that Connie stood on her hind legs and struck out over the line.

The instant her front leg was over the line, she knew she was in full control. Whirling away from us, she fled as fast as she could. I had to let go of the thirty-foot line and stood frozen in my tracks, paralyzed with fear. With the blanket waving on her flanks, Connie ran through the trees like a deer in full flight, thirty feet of line waving behind her and threatening to wrap around a tree or a bush with every stride she took. My heart was in my mouth. I didn't think she'd be able to negotiate the hundred yards back to the stable without hitting a tree, which would likely injure her severely or even kill her.

What happened next was truly memorable. La Confédération didn't even touch a tree. She ran straight to her box stall, somehow crossing the cobblestones and passing through the door without so much as a hesitation. This was the same door she'd refused to walk through just two days before. Tex and I ran to the stable as fast as our legs could carry us, listening for sounds that would indicate she'd hit the back wall of her stall—she had, after all, negotiated the door at full speed. Tex, thirty years my junior and fit as a trout, reached the stable while I was only about halfway there. I slowed down and listened for some report from him as I approached. Thankfully, he told me Connie was OK.

At that moment I wanted a chance to deal with every atheist on earth. I wanted to ask them how what we'd just witnessed could have happened without a God in heaven. We inspected Connie and there wasn't a sign that she'd hit the wall. Once she'd settled, she looked for all the world exactly as she had before the incident. I stripped her down, Tex gave her a sponge bath, and we allowed her some time to drink and eat a bit of hay. Meanwhile, we discussed our next move.

"I want some livestock panels, like the ones we used as wings earlier this morning while schooling at the van. We had four of them near the truck but I'll need eight when I'm ready for my next session," I said.

Tex said no problem, he'd make sure they were near the gate by one o'clock.

We went back to the riders' café for lunch, La Confédération and I were once again the subject of heated conversation. Bets were being laid on whether I would succeed, and Tex was acting as translator, filling me in on the discussions as best he could. I had gone from severely concerned to highly confident and back again in one twenty-four-hour period. While I choked down a sandwich, Tex told me that from the beginning he'd figured I would probably get the stall and the truck done, but he seriously doubted there was any way I'd succeed with the starting gate.

Just after one, I walked Connie back to the permanent training gate with Tex following with the blanket. At the rear end of the stall we had created an enclosure with four of the eight livestock panels. The other four made a similar enclosure in front of the wooden structure. I waited until I had entered the rear enclosure to put the protective blanket on Connie. Should she get loose again, our enclosures would prevent another death-defying trip through the trees. The only way out was through the gate.

It was quite a maze, that hourglass-like setup, but I was pleased to know that my filly was safe. Connie was a basket case when I asked her to pass through the gate, but, just as we'd conquered the stable door, so too did we emerge victorious over the training gate. I stopped for a moment to silently thank Dayflower for showing me how to use the panel system. By three thirty or so, I could walk Connie calmly through the gate and even back her through it while standing six to eight feet in front of her. This allowed her to think quietly through the act of walking or backing through the pair of wooden walls.

The goal for day three was to re-establish her confidence in the training gate with her tack in place. We accomplished this before the breakfast break. This time, the café conversations were quite different. I still couldn't understand French, but a handshake and a slap on the back mean the same thing the world over. Tex remained cautious. He reminded me that the regulation starting gate was still waiting in the forest, about half a mile away.

After breakfast, I put him up on La Confédération. Her progress was dramatic. Tex was able to walk her through the wooden gate, stand her in it with both gates closed and even back her in without a problem. The next step was to open the enclosures and work once again from the ground without a rider. We finished the third day with Tex up and no support from the panels. When we had Connie standing quietly in the starting gate with the gates closed in front and behind, we stroked her and talked to her and could see that her comfort levels had definitely increased. The training gate was becoming a safe place in her mind.

At dawn on day four, Tex and I went to examine the regulation starting gate. Finding no particular surprises, I suggested that we repeat each of our procedures once more before lunch, and then go to the metal gate that afternoon. The morning went beautifully. Connie performed without a glitch.

At lunch, skepticism was again running high. Most of the riders thought the regulation gate would prove to be the impassable hurdle.

We finally approached the metal gate in the woods after lunch with another rider on a quiet saddle horse along for company. What would La Confédération think?

No way was this filly going anywhere near the dreaded regulation gate! She flew into a rage. Tex managed to stay on board, I'm not sure how, as Connie exploded. Bucking, rearing and trying to bolt in four different directions at once, she scored 10 out of 10 for endangering herself and very nearly decapitated me with a front foot. Clearly, we needed another step in the transition to the regulation gate. Back to the drawing board we went. How in the world was I going to get this filly anywhere near that metal contraption?

As the lessons of Prince of Darkness, Dayflower and many others bounced through my brain, I had a thought: what if we got a tractor to pull the regulation gate from where it was to a point just in front of the training gate? I knew I could control Connie in the wooden structure. If I could get her to stand quietly inside and then open the gate, I might get her to walk forward out of the training gate and into the metal one. We could reconstruct the two circular enclosures at either end so that the front one would sit just ahead of the regulation gate. That would ensure a safe environment.

It worked. Within a half hour or so, Connie was walking through both the wooden and metal gates with Tex on her back. We finished day four by repeating the procedure fifty to sixty times. I'd figured out the kind of environment Connie required, and she was enlightening me with every step. Before our session ended, she was calmly standing inside the metal gate while we stroked her and told her how wonderful she was. I explained to Tex that all horses fear the unfamiliar but are seldom afraid of something they understand, so long as it doesn't hurt them.

Day five was dedicated to gradually separating the metal structure from the wooden one, four to five feet at a time. We used panels to create a hallway between the two structures, and by the end of the day, we could ride La Confédération straight into the regulation gate. Many of the riders watched us in amazement.

On day six, we asked La Confédération to accept the regulation gate in its original position, half a mile away in the woods. We took some time to school her without a rider but, eventually, we were successful. Tex could ride her in and out of the gate, and we could close them up and even put the saddle horse in beside her. I was sore and beat up after one of the most grueling weeks of my life, but the satisfaction I felt overrode it all.

On the afternoon of the seventh day, André Fabre rode a saddle horse through the woods to the regulation starting gate and watched as La Confédération quietly walked in and out of it, first with me leading and then just she and her rider. She was wearing her training halter and her protective blanket. Four other Thoroughbreds were ridden from the training yard to our location, and they and Connie were loaded into the gate just as they would be at the races. Connie stood calmly as a couple of them acted up, and when the gates opened, she raced up the course, leading the other four. A pride-filled lump formed in my throat.

We held a little party at the riders' café that evening, and you can't imagine the carryings-on. Tex was overjoyed and made sure the rest of the party knew it. I left Chantilly the following morning, confident that La Confédération would become a successful racehorse.

About a month later, I got a call from a former student of mine, Rupert Pritchard-Gordon. He was at the track where La Confédération had just raced and won easily. Tex was there with him. I was delighted. It was no surprise to me that she could run; but for her to come through all those phobias and graduate with an easy win at a major French track was gratifying to the tenth power. I congratulated Tex and asked him to keep me informed about Connie's progress.

About a month after that, I got another call from Rupert, but this one was very different from the first.

"It was horrible, Monty," he said. "She didn't want to enter the gate, and then when she did, she fought while inside. She eventually stood on her hind legs and bashed the gates open with her front feet, throwing the jockey into them. He was injured and she broke free and ran up the racecourse. She was disqualified and is now suspended from racing."

Words can't describe how I felt at this news. I couldn't imagine what had caused such an intelligent horse to relapse. I immediately called Anthony Stroud in Sheikh Mohammed's office and told him I wanted to see the racetrack videotape of the incident. I wanted to assess the circumstances surrounding the disaster.

The tape arrived within three days, and when I watched it I felt angrier than I've ever been. The tape showed La Confédération being led toward the starting gate without her protective blanket and with my special training halter upside down. Her handler was a man I didn't recognize. As she approached the gate, Connie was reluctant to go near it without her blanket in place. A race attendant appeared with a long buggy whip and several men restrained her as she was whipped across the hind legs. They got her in, but as soon as the rails touched her flanks, the same way the stable door had done, she flew into a rage.

I watched La Confédération kick out and then rear, striking the gates open. She flew out of the metal contraption and up the racecourse, running for her very life. The injured jockey was removed from the gate and taken away. I sat staring at the blank screen when the tape ended, trying to control the anger welling up inside me. I called Anthony Stroud and reported what I'd seen. I told him I would never go near another horse of theirs if they didn't remove La Confédération from France immediately and get her to Newmarket where she could be placed with someone who would follow my procedures to the letter.

With that conversation behind me, I called Rupert, who by this time was well aware of the circumstances surrounding the incident. Rupert told me that the decision had been made to run Connie on that day even though

Tex was on holiday. She had been doing so well, they were sure she'd be just fine. Someone untrained was assigned to take her to the starting gate. He didn't know how to put her halter and blanket on, so he decided to leave the blanket off, which contributed to the disaster.

This incident illustrates what often happens with remedial horses. Some people tend to regard horses in much the same way as they do machinery. If it's broken, they want it fixed; when it's fixed, it's supposed to work. The people around La Confédération had been lulled into a sense of security by her good behavior.

Anthony Stroud and Sheikh Mohammed immediately agreed to send La Confédération to Newmarket, where I went to work with her as soon as she was settled in her new surroundings. It took very little time to regain all the lost ground, and the proper procedures were followed throughout the balance of her career. I visited Connie several times while she was racing. She ultimately earned $119,203 and was an internationally approved Group winner in England. She retired from racing in 1995 and is currently raising babies in Kentucky.

The third in this trio of outstanding Thoroughbred females that came to me in rapid succession was Song of Africa. She was in Florida when I first met her and had been banned from racing after causing injuries to several people and destroying a starting gate. Dozens of horsemen on the Florida racing scene said she was an impossible case, but the lessons of Dayflower and La Confédération carried me to a successful conclusion with her, too. Before she was retired as a broodmare, Song of Africa won six races, including an internationally approved stake, and amassed earnings of $223,538.

The respect I feel for horses such as Dayflower, La Confédération and Song of Africa and the education I gained from them are virtually impossible to measure. The horseman who fails to take advantage of the potential for learning presented by these wonderful individuals is missing out on one of life's great experiences.

DUALLY

Pepinics Dually, or Dually for short, was a gem. A bay Quarter Horse of just 14.3 hands and 1,250 pounds, he was a very strong, world-class reined cow horse and Triple Crown Champion for the National Reined Cow Horse Association in 1994. He was bred by Greg Ward, with whom I was at college in the mid-1950s. I bought Dually after Greg had already shown him, but I had a world of fun training him during the time when Greg and his son John won several championships with him.

My special training halter is named after him, a legacy of his importance to me. I designed it while he was my personal riding horse. The Dually halter is based on an old idea of Don Dodge's—Don, my former teacher, called it the come-along—and it has become a large part of my training life, assisting me and other horsemen around the world. It was the palomino stallion Barlet who really showed me the need for a specifically designed halter. The come-along had to be fashioned from a long rope, but using it helped Barlet change from an angry, vicious stallion to a cooperative equine partner. Now there are approximately 120,000 Dually halters in existence. When properly handled, they connect handlers and horses far more closely than other types of halters.

When my first book, *The Man Who Listens to Horses*, was published in September 1996, my British publisher asked me to do a book launch tour, giving demonstrations of join-up and signing copies of the book. They'd heard me describing the Quarter Horse I loved so much back home and thought it would be a great idea to bring Dually along on the tour. In addition to demonstrating join-up, I could show Dually working cattle and performing all the maneuvers required in his discipline: sliding stops, spins and flying lead changes. They wanted British audiences, who were unfamiliar with Western shows and rodeo, to get a glimpse of the skills we'd developed in our horses in the western United States.

So we got out Dually's passport and booked his airfare. After his quarantine, we made the trip together, although we very nearly didn't go. I had contracted a dangerous type of pneumonia and my doctor forbade me to travel. There was no way I wasn't going—this was a big moment for me; my life story was being published. I was booked in twenty cities and towns across the British Isles, including six stops in Ireland, and Dually was ready

Dually performs a beautiful stop with a loose rein, 1996. It gave me great pleasure to ride this Triple Crown Champion Working Cow Horse.

to go. I knocked back three times the recommended dose of my prescription and boarded a KLM plane to Amsterdam.

During the flight I felt so ill I couldn't sit next to another person, so I left my seat, ducked through the little door at the back and curled up next to Dually in the hold. My lungs were half full of liquid and my temperature was off the scale. I was close to passing out but I received such solace from the calm presence of Dually that I made it through. We made it to Amsterdam, but that flight was one of the few times in my life when I had good reason to think I was going to die.

From Amsterdam, Dually and I rode a truck to Calais and took the ferry across to Dover. After another three-hour truck ride, my health had improved and we were ready to begin the tour.

Dually was an instant hit with the fans. For him, we created an oval arena, larger than those I used for my other demonstrations. Half a dozen steers would be released into the pen and I'd put him through his paces. I'd identify the steer I wanted to cut out of the group and Dually would go about his business. Once separated from his buddies, the steer would naturally try to rejoin them. With no cues from me, Dually would make incredible dives and spins to keep the steer separated from the others. The audience, who'd never seen this kind of thing before, were amazed.

We decided to add a bit of humor to our program with one of the girls who were working for us on the tour. She'd go into the ring and stand at one end with her back to the fence. Her job was simple: all she had to do was get to the other side any way she could. Dually stopped her every time.

Meanwhile, I was proud to see the lines of people after the demonstrations, asking to have their copies of the book signed. It brought me such an amazing feeling of acceptance after all the years in which I had had to keep quiet about my work.

The highlight of the tour was receiving a message from the Queen. She was interested in seeing the presentation with Dually and asked me to conduct a private showing at Windsor Castle for herself and Princess Margaret.

So Dually took me back to Windsor Castle, where this new life of mine had begun. I believe Dually is the first, last and only horse ever to work cattle in the riding hall at Windsor Castle. The Queen and Princess Margaret enjoyed watching him very much, and I will always remember standing with Her Majesty for a photograph with this wonderful gelding that gave me so much pleasure.

Dually died in 2001 of an incurable joint disease, which took him from me all too young. In retrospect, I think I probably retired him from competition too early for him to reach his full potential. He willingly became my private riding horse while in the prime of his life, a time when he might have preferred more activity. But he remained a cooperative, generous partner until the very end. He's buried at Flag Is Up near Johnny Tivio, Night Mist and Julia's Doll.

NUEBE

To date, we've conducted over 1,200 public demonstrations in fifteen years and we've never had to cancel one, or even start late. There have been some close calls: snow in Las Vegas knocked our tent down and almost stopped us, and delayed flights put other demonstrations in jeopardy. But each time the show went on.

Every horse that took part in our demonstrations was improved, even if a few could be considered only slightly better. The vast majority, however, were dramatically changed before the eyes of more than a million people in total. It is impossible to remember every horse brought to me, and just as impossible to forget some of them.

In May 2002, we were in Munich. At one o'clock in the afternoon we were examining the horses on offer for our demonstration later that day, to make sure they were sound and healthy. My rider of five years, Jason Davis, was putting the horses through the round pen to give the veterinarian a chance to watch them trot. I was in the stands, speaking with the owners to decide which horses would provide the best educational demonstrations. I had four categories to fill: the untrained horse, the horse with incorrigible ground manners, the bucker and the horse that refused to load in the trailer.

Nuebe, a six-year-old black stallion, was led into the round pen, and as Jason began to do a health and fitness test, I greeted the two ladies who owned him. They were both in their forties, and their clothes, demeanor and conversation spoke volumes about their experience in the horse world. They were, in fact, professional trainers of dressage horses. They told me that Nuebe could easily be a world-class competition horse except for his deep fear of umbrellas.

"What?" I asked. "Did I hear you right? He's frightened of umbrellas?"

Yes, they said. About a year before, one of them had been riding Nuebe in a competition in the Munich area. Summer thunderstorms are common in that part of the world and while Nuebe was performing, a downpour moved in. Everyone started to pop open their umbrellas, including a man who was standing next to the rail, causing Nuebe to run through the show grounds in a panic, ultimately injuring himself and his rider. Since then, no one had been able to get near him with an umbrella, no matter how hard they tried.

I asked the owners if they had an umbrella with them. They did, but for obvious reasons they were keeping the "horrible instrument" hidden under their chairs. I asked one of my assistants to take it out but to be careful. We remained outside the round pen and opened the umbrella just a little. Nuebe went ballistic. He blasted around the pen, tugging at the lead and rearing into the air while trumpeting through his nose like a bull elephant. His response was as dramatic as any I've ever witnessed. I could see that Nuebe would probably injure himself if we persisted, so we quickly folded up the umbrella and put it back under the seats.

I politely thanked the owners and marked down Nuebe as unsuitable for a public demonstration. I moved on to the next horse.

When every horse had completed his trip to the round pen, I decided which ones I wanted for the show. I was about to tell Jason when he said, "You can do him, you know."

"I can do who?" I asked.

"The black horse. You can fix him."

"Are you out of your mind?" I said. "I have a sold-out building with five thousand seats and you want me to do a horse like that? I've never dealt with an umbrella phobia in my life, and it seems to me to be incredibly risky. I'd be inviting disaster."

Jason looked at me with a wry smile and a twinkle in his eye. "You can do him, Monty. It might be a great demonstration, and I'm convinced you'll get him to accept the umbrella."

Working to overcome Nuebe's phobia in Munich, Germany, 2001

Somewhere inside me I did want to work with that horse, but without Jason's encouragement I would never have taken the chance. I agreed to include Nuebe in the second phase of the evening's demonstration. It would be risky, but we had to give it a try.

When Nuebe came into the ring that night, the audience collectively gasped at his beauty. With the house lights off and the round pen bathed in heavy stage lights, his coat shone like polished onyx and his carriage was regal. During join-up, Nuebe soon came to see me as a friendly partner in an otherwise strange world of lights and sounds. Five thousand people sat on the edge of their seats, waiting to see what would happen next.

Jason brought the umbrella into the pen. Although it was fully closed, Nuebe put on a show that froze every spectator. I told the audience the story behind his strange phobia. Jason opened the umbrella, and Nuebe frantically tried to get as far away from it as he could. Sand flew through the air and reached people well up into the stands. His eyes were like saucers and his nostrils flared wide open, blowing hot breath.

I asked Jason to close the umbrella and began to walk around the round pen, wondering just what the heck I would do. I needed Nuebe to trust me, so I worked hard to get my adrenaline and pulse rate down. Then I began to school him using the Dually halter until he could understand and respect it. My next step was to take out the artificial arm I use. Fashioned out of a rake handle, an old sleeve and glove and stuffed with sponge, it allows me to work with phobic horses while remaining at a safe distance from dangerous hoofs. I'm sure that for Nuebe my invention resembled an umbrella. It was larger but didn't open, and soon he was letting me rub his body with it as I used the full complement of the language of equus to tell him that I intended him no harm. I did my best to let him know that he was safe with me and that I would protect him from all killer umbrellas.

After about ten minutes, Jason brought me the umbrella, which I held close to the arm as I continued the discussion I'd begun with Nuebe. Within three or four minutes, he was accepting the arm and the umbrella together. Next, I sent the arm out of the ring and continued my work with just the umbrella. Within a minute or so, Nuebe was letting me massage his body with the thing he dreaded most. He was sweating and trembling but trying hard to believe in me. This was what join-up was able to achieve. Perhaps more than ever before, I felt that I was on the right track, that we could dramatically improve the relationship between man and horse.

I opened the large umbrella slightly and massaged Nuebe with the loose material, promising him with my actions that there'd be no pain. Slowly, I opened it more and more, and Nuebe's trust in me gradually overcame his fear. I could hear my audience beginning to murmur to one another, and I realized I was still surrounded by five thousand people. I hadn't heard a sound from them for the past fifteen minutes or so. With the umbrella wide open, I began to move it around Nuebe. While he was clearly troubled, he didn't run away.

Gradually I began to move around the pen, opening and closing the umbrella and holding it high over my head. The lead line was attached to the Dually halter, but Nuebe was following me without tugging on it.

At that point I thought about thanking the audience and ending that segment of the evening. But I decided to go a bit further, as the thought of Jason and his twinkling eye came to my mind. I reached out, unsnapped the line from the halter and tossed it out of the way, toward the gate. Then I moved in a large circle with the umbrella fully open and raised over my head. Nuebe followed me, as if he were saying, "Yes, I can do it. I can overcome this phobia."

What happened next was a first for me, and it certainly hasn't happened since that night. The soundman turned the music up and the audience began to clap in time. Nuebe was frightened by the audience's response, but it only served to bring him closer to me. As I walked faster, Nuebe picked up his pace in order to stay close to me even though I had the "horrible instrument" fully open. The audience began to applaud, and Nuebe and I received a standing ovation that went on for two to three minutes.

I thanked everyone and asked for silence so I could continue. I began to rub Nuebe between the eyes and around the head as a gesture of appreciation for the courage he'd shown. I walked once more around the ring, umbrella open and umbrella closed, in order to give Nuebe a chance to come down from what had been a very traumatic experience for him. I sensed his adrenaline level dropping. The demonstration was over.

As Nuebe left the arena, the audience sprang to their feet and gave us another standing ovation. Many stomped the floor, whistled and called out in appreciation.

As a child, I'd been fearful of the objects my father had used to punish me. Whips, ropes, even polo mallets were frightening, just as umbrellas were for Nuebe. He'd needed to find trust, affection and understanding. He'd needed to know that he was safe from violence and bodily harm. Join-up gave him that trust. I felt huge pride and, at the same time, humility at the incredible demonstration of the power of the language I call equus.

SHY BOY

This is a book about the horses in my life, and so although Shy Boy has a book of his own, *Shy Boy: The Horse That Came In from the Wild*, it's essential that he be included here, too.

Once I had gained some recognition from the general public for my work, I began to receive various requests from the media. One of these was from the BBC in London, asking if I had any idea of how they might make a program that would explain my concepts to a wider audience, not just horse people.

By now I had laid to rest the lack of acceptance from my father and others. After all, I could prove my theories were effective and had done so in front of thousands of people in countless towns and cities around the world, and my book was an international best seller. If I wanted acceptance and approval of my ideas, I had more than anyone could wish for. Yet there was one thing from my past that I hadn't laid to rest. It was the time I'd gone out into the wilderness, up in the high ranges of Nevada, and achieved join-up with Buster. As I described earlier, when I'd ridden Buster back to the ranch, the cowboys suggested I'd found a mustang that had already been ridden. They just didn't believe what I'd done. It still bothered me. I had been so full of pride and excitement that day and no one had believed me.

I suggested to the BBC that I could try to do the same thing again, and the cameras would be there to see what happened. I would try to perform join-up in the wild. The BBC loved the idea and began making the arrangements.

Dr. Robert Miller, veterinarian and renowned animal behaviorist, was hired to act as a referee of sorts. He would verify the legitimacy of the mustang and the procedures, and would ensure the horse was properly cared for. As well, he'd be available for any medical needs that might arise. Lawrence Scanlan, the editor of my first book, would come along as an observer.

Our first step was to adopt a wild mustang from the Bureau of Land Management, the federal agency that controls wild horses in the United States. I called him Shy Boy. An independent observer from the Santa Barbara Wildlife Care Network was named by the BBC to represent them as a referee. She selected a neutral, well-fenced pasture site for Shy Boy, where he remained until he was returned to the wilderness. I was careful to have no contact with him whatsoever, so that he would remain completely wild.

There I was, forty years older, up in the high desert, just me and this wild mustang, with no ropes, no fences, nothing—oh, except a film crew. That gave it a different feel, for sure, but there was going to be no disputing what happened this time. Every bit of my work would be recorded in living color.

Shy Boy joined up with me in exactly twenty-four hours, as I had predicted he would several months earlier in London. Here was a wild horse, choosing to be with me rather than to flee into the thousands of acres of wilderness that beckoned in every direction. I had a halter and surcingle (bellyband) on him in thirty-six hours. Each step of the plan stayed within a few hours of the schedule. Within seventy-two hours, I had a rider on Shy Boy's back and he was cantering along following our saddle horses. Independent observers verified every step. Join-up between man and horse worked, even in the wild.

The documentary was shown around the world over the next three years or so, and there are still skeptics who don't believe what I did. Psychologists could describe the relationship forged between Shy Boy and me as I followed him through the backcountry as catastrophic bonding. This term describes what often takes place when planes crash in mountainous terrain or hikers get lost in the backcountry: we come together in the face of grave danger. It seems we all take on a herd mentality when we perceive our lives to be at risk. I absolutely fell in love with Shy Boy during those seven to ten days when we created the documentary.

After the BBC left California, I took Shy Boy to a student of mine, Ron Ralls, for further training as a working cow horse while I traveled the world promoting *The Man Who Listens to Horses.* Shy Boy took his lessons well and became an even-tempered, cooperative equine student.

Journalists and readers often asked about Shy Boy. People wanted to know where he was and how he was doing, and many asked the same question: "What do you think Shy Boy would do if you took him back out to the wilderness and released him with the same herd of horses?" My answer was, "I don't know." I didn't think anyone had ever tried that before, and so no one could really know the answer. I was interested to find out.

Eleven months after Shy Boy's and my first adventure, we set out to film another documentary. The plan was to return to the place where the first one had been filmed, release Shy Boy when we found his herd, and see what his response would be. I was convinced the other horses would kick him out immediately. He had been eating domestic feed and drinking water from a different area, so his body would give off a totally different scent from that of the family group.

I was wrong. They took him back in as if he'd been away for just a day or so. Not one of them said a negative word to him. It was about three o'clock in the afternoon when we released him, and by dark he was miles from us with his herd. I told everyone in the film crew that he would come back either in the night or first thing in the morning. I actually felt certain we would see him around our campsite at dawn.

I was wrong again. At daylight he was nowhere to be seen. But at about nine o'clock he turned up on top of a hill about a quarter of a mile from our location. He stopped for a few seconds, looked back at the other horses and then cantered down off the hill and directly to me. It was one of the most moving experiences of my life.

Shy Boy was home to stay, and he has never been away from us since that moment. He lives on Flag Is Up Farms and I feel certain he believes he owns the place. Pat rides him as much as anyone does, and his regular job is to escort young horses to and from the riding arenas and training track on our farm. He shows young Thoroughbreds how to go through the starting gate and is quite capable of assisting young cutting horses or reined cow horses by helping with the duties of controlling the cattle they are working.

Shy Boy is one of the gentlest horses on the face of this earth. When the documentaries are being aired across the country, I'm often asked by the television producers to assist in their promotion. I usually take Shy Boy with me to the television studios. He walks over the cables and under the spotlights. I also take him to events where children come to meet him, and he seems to have a great time. Shy Boy loves children and they certainly love him. We have a special blanket he wears with his name on it, and it works in conjunction with a very effective diaper. He also sports four rubber hoof jackets, which prevent him from slipping on floors made for people.

One time we took Shy Boy along on a demonstration tour of the northwest United States because five public television studios and some affiliates wanted him to be present for the airing of the documentaries. He made appearances in Medford, Oregon; Seattle and Yakima, Washington; Ogden, Utah; and Denver. In Yakima, for a morning show, Jason Davis, my

Shy Boy racing the wind in 1998

rider and assistant at the time, prepared Shy Boy and, at the agreed moment, led him in and presented him to the host, who was interviewing me. We were engaged in a great conversation when I heard a strange sound coming from around Shy Boy's rear legs. I couldn't look back to see what was going on, but suddenly a familiar smell began to permeate the air of the studio. When we cut for a commercial, I turned to see Jason, red-faced, coming in with a shovel and a black plastic bag. He looked at me sheepishly and said that he had forgotten to zip up the bottom of Shy Boy's diaper. The staff of that television studio are probably still telling stories about our visit.

In San Antonio, Texas, at a meeting of grammar school principals from all over the United States, I was a keynote speaker and Shy Boy was my sidekick. There were six thousand people in one room in a huge convention center and no opportunity for a rehearsal. We just had to get on with it. Shy Boy and I proceeded down the center aisle toward a very large stage, which fortunately had a wheelchair ramp at one end. The mustang walked up the ramp, right out to the center of the stage, where he stood, ears up, viewing his audience. Shy Boy had no idea why he was receiving a standing ovation, but he remained totally calm as six thousand people produced deafening applause.

At the conclusion of our presentation, Shy Boy walked back down the ramp and stood quietly while literally thousands of people came to say hello to him. I've known a lot of horses in my time, but I don't believe I've ever seen one that could have tolerated this environment with the tranquility exhibited by Shy Boy.

The most recent important event in Shy Boy's life involved the Rose Bowl Parade on January 1, 2003. The officials of the enormous event asked me to take part to represent the work I do with horses. The Rose Bowl Parade is a New Year's Day tradition in Pasadena, California, where it has taken place for over a hundred years and is the warm-up to the grandfather of all college football games, the Rose Bowl.

The parade begins at about eight thirty in the morning and follows a five-mile route down Colorado Boulevard. Approximately one million people are on site to view it, and the air force entertains the crowd with low flyovers in stealth bombers. A large portion of the parade is made up of huge floats, each playing its own music, and the city is filled with a mixture of utterly unique sounds. Marching bands and baton-twirling beauties compete for rousing applause as the parade moves along at about two and a half miles per hour.

This year the parade officials wanted to pay tribute to the American mustang—and I had the most famous American mustang in the world. I was excited about the prospect of being part of the massive extravaganza and was confident that Shy Boy could handle the incredible challenge the parade would present. Then the officials told me they wanted six mustangs to be involved, some to come from Indian reservations as well as from the Bureau of Land Management. This meant we would have to train five wild mustangs in only five months.

Shy Boy proved extremely helpful in the process of educating the recently captured horses. Jason was the primary trainer, because I was on the road virtually the whole time the horses were being prepared. I can claim very little credit for getting them ready to face one of the most daunting environments any horse has ever met.

At 14.1 hands and 950 pounds, Shy Boy is a bit on the small side to look appropriate under me in a parade, so we decided Pat should ride him. Linda Klausner, the equine coordinator for the parade, filled us in on what we should expect. We would follow a float called "The Candy Man." Huge and festively decorated, it was designed to attract the attention of children, and in fact children would lean out from every part of it, throwing candy to the masses of people as we moved along. The float that would follow us was a twenty-foot dragon that would roar every twenty seconds or so and blow huge amounts of steam from its nostrils, each of which was about two feet in diameter.

Linda told us that a favorite pastime of youngsters at the parade was to throw firecrackers under the horses passing by. "Cherry bombs will be rolled out into the street and they will go off, making a very loud explosion," she said. Confetti and ticker tape would be thrown from the buildings and many of the horses would be spooked by the jet aircraft flying low.

Jason, Pat and other members of the farm staff literally turned our indoor arena into a house of horrors to get the horses ready for the parade. They hung balloons, plastic tarpaulins and mannequins from the rafters and set off fireworks to simulate the pandemonium the horses would soon experience.

On December 31, we had to be in the staging area by ten at night so we could start saddling around four thirty the next morning and make sure our tack and costumes were in order for the six thirty departure. We rode to the start, about two miles away, and the horses performed admirably with Shy Boy showing them the way. I rode Navajo, a mustang that stands nearly 16 hands and weighs about 1,200 pounds. While he was not as comfortable with his surroundings as Shy Boy, he behaved very well.

All six horses completed the five miles without a single negative step. I think Sammy Davis Jr.'s recording of "The Candy Man" will ring in our ears for the rest of our days. Shy Boy seemed to know he had done a good job when we arrived at the schoolyard at the end of Colorado Boulevard, the designated finishing point for the equestrian participants. Even though it had been a grueling day, he seemed to have more spring in his step than any of the other horses and let Pat know that he wanted to be ridden in and around them to tell them what a proud teacher he was. I, too, was proud of them all.

Today, Shy Boy has his own box stall for sleeping and a field for daily turnouts. Literally hundreds of people visit him every week. He has a home here for the rest of his life, and my relationship with him is as close as I've had with any horse. Shy Boy is a wonderful little American mustang and a great tribute to those survivors of the early Spanish settlers in the western part of the United States.

JOHNNY TIVIO

I have left the most important horse in my life until last. Telling Johnny Tivio's story takes me back to the days when I was younger and stronger. At the age of seventy, with five vertebrae welded together, I often think how wonderful it was that Johnny Tivio and I enjoyed the prime of our lives with one another.

Johnny Tivio was a blood bay Quarter Horse stallion born on April 24, 1956. He was the result of mating Poco Tivio with a Green Cattle Company mare wearing the R O brand. She was small and had been raised near the California town of Chowchilla. I suppose that's how she came by the name Chowchilla Peewee. In the early days of the state of California, the Green Cattle Company was an enormous ranching operation that spread from the top of California near Oregon all the way down into Mexico, and its registered brand was R O. Charles Araujo of Coalinga, California, acquired Chowchilla Peewee in the 1940s. I don't suppose anybody knew her actual breeding. Her registration papers only came into existence when an inspection process allowed horses to be registered as Quarter Horses. Apparently Chowchilla Peewee met the criteria and so she received a number.

Charles Araujo sold Johnny Tivio as a yearling to a man from Bakersfield, California, by the name of Carl Williams. Mr. Williams was not a professional horseman but he had property near the trainer Bob Mettler, who started Johnny Tivio at two years of age. When a different trainer moved into the neighborhood, Carl Williams, for one reason or another, sent Johnny Tivio to him.

The second trainer, who shall remain nameless, decided to enter Johnny Tivio in competition, starting early in his third year, and not just in one but in two separate disciplines, the hackamore and the cutting. Johnny won no championships in those early days but, he caught the eye of every professional who watched him work. While not beautifully conformed, Johnny had a coat of hair that was like burnished bronze, one of the most gorgeous seen anywhere. He had an outstanding head and neck and moved like the consummate athlete he would turn out to be.

The second trainer was not one to be too serious about his responsibilities, and most of the professionals I traveled with thought his treatment of the horse was less than he deserved. Johnny Tivio's age put him square in line to compete with my prospect Fiddle D'Or in 1960. While I worked hard to give Fiddle every opportunity to maximize his efforts, Johnny Tivio was not given the same consideration. Pat would often say to me, "Man, you're lucky Johnny Tivio is being trained by this particular fellow. I don't think Fiddle could ever beat him if a responsible trainer was in charge."

By midsummer, Pat and I were on the circuit. As I recall, I was showing My Blue Heaven in the open working cow horse class and Fiddle D'Or in the hackamore. We arrived one night in Watsonville, California. Just outside the town, on the road to the fairgrounds, we drove by a honky-tonk saloon and Pat pointed to it.

"Look at that truck over there," she said. "That's the guy who's showing Johnny Tivio."

The truck was full of horses. It was the type of vehicle used to haul cattle, often referred to as slat-sided, so you could see the animals through the walls. I was appalled that any trainer would make his horse stand outside a bar while he drank. I must say, however, that I was not terribly surprised given the person involved.

We drove on to the fairgrounds, unloaded our horses, watered them and gave them twenty minutes of walking and trotting, since they'd just completed a five-hour journey. We housed them in their assigned stalls with comfortable beds and food and water. Unhooking the trailer, we headed back to town to check in at our hotel. I believe it was around nine thirty when we passed the saloon for the second time. The truck was still there and the horses were still inside.

The next morning we were up at about five to get ready for the preliminary competition, which was to begin around eight o'clock. On the fairgrounds, we cleaned, fed and watered our horses, giving them a chance to collect themselves before we began to tack up. Pat went to the horse-show office to do the normal paperwork and pick up our numbers. Walking back to our stable, she noticed that the stalls allocated to Johnny Tivio's trainer were still empty.

Around seven we began to saddle up, and as long as I live I will never forget what we saw in the next half hour. The stables were located at the

Pure reining: Johnny and me on our way to victory

bottom of a hill and the approach road was quite steep. We watched as the truck we recognized from the saloon came roaring down the hill. It came to a stop near the arena and the trainer got out on the driver's side. A rather disheveled-looking woman got out on the other.

The trainer lowered the ramp and I recognized each of the horses he unloaded and tied to the side of the truck, including Johnny Tivio. The trainer threw the saddles on immediately and then led them one by one to a large communal water trough, allowing them to drink their fill. As you can imagine, each took a large quantity of water—they'd just spent the night without a sip. The trainer tied them back to the side of the truck, with the exception of Johnny Tivio. He put a hackamore on Johnny and climbed into the saddle. Then he grabbed the woman by the arm and swung her up just behind him. "Hang on," he said, and into the arena they went at a full canter, her arms wrapped around his middle like a passenger on a motorcycle. For the next ten minutes or so he navigated the arena, introducing his new friend to other trainers, cantering, stopping and spinning Johnny Tivio, to give her a thrilling ride.

I told Pat that there was no way Johnny Tivio could beat us today, and remarked on how sad it was that Fiddle D'Or was getting an unfair advantage over a superior opponent. We competed in the preliminaries and at the end of the day, both horses made it to the finals. To my amazement, Fiddle D'Or finished second and Johnny Tivio won the class! Fiddle didn't finish second very many times. I won the world championship with Fiddle D'Or that season not because he was the world's best but because the world's best was not given the opportunity to prove himself.

After the Watsonville incident, I said to Pat, "I want to own that horse someday. The world should know just how good he really is."

They didn't campaign Johnny Tivio in the hackamore in 1961, and the field was left to Fiddle. Johnny was shown sparingly and mostly in the cutting. Irresponsibility was costing this trainer, and we got word that Carl Williams was taking Johnny home for extended periods of time. Throughout the 1961 and 1962 seasons, I saw Carl Williams on several occasions, and each time I mentioned that if Johnny was ever for sale, I would be seriously interested. In the autumn of 1962, the situation came to a head in King City, California.

A citizen reported that a truck had been parked for two days with animals inside. There didn't appear to be any food or water available and the animals needed urgent care. The authorities broke in and discovered that the truck was registered to Carl Williams. They went to his house with the intention of charging him with animal cruelty, only to find that the truck had been in the hands of the trainer. Although other horses had been aboard, Johnny Tivio was the only one that belonged to Carl Williams.

Mr. Williams remembered our earlier conversations and called me to let me know the time had come for a parting of the ways with the trainer. He wanted to sell Johnny Tivio. I immediately went over and made the transaction. George A. Smith, a client of mine, bought him with me in partnership, and I held the option to buy out Mr. Smith. The price was $6,000, and to me that seemed an absolute steal. However, Carl Williams told me that because of all the neglect, Johnny Tivio had suffered acute laminitis and the vets would not give him a clean report as a competition horse. They thought he could function normally for breeding.

When I arrived at the stable, I was shocked to see Johnny's condition. He was 150 pounds underweight and his front feet were low in the heel and elongated by about 30 percent. On the X-rays, however, the skeletal changes seemed minimal. Johnny's gorgeous coat was now dull. Still, we held out great hopes that, with proper foot care and nutrition, we could get him back in the show ring.

I took my time getting acquainted with Johnny, allowing him to tell me when he was ready for physical activity. My farrier, J. R. Jennings, did a remarkable job getting those front feet back in working order. Each evening I found myself excitedly discussing this new member of our family with Pat. I thought he had more natural ability than any horse I had ever seen.

By April of 1964, the luster was back in Johnny Tivio's coat. There was a spring in his step and a new pair of front feet with which to dance through his routines as no horse before him could. I knew his performances by heart from the previous three years, and what I saw coming from him now was a new level of excellence, far above his performance at Watsonville or any of the other competitions. We were beginning to work together as a team, and I was experiencing a very special partnership with him.

The day came for the entries to close for the 1964 Salinas competition.

Johnny and me winning a cutting championship

Other than the Grand National finals, Salinas was the granddaddy event for working cow horses. Before entering Salinas, I remember calling Pat to the arena one day, saying, "Watch Johnny and tell me whether I should enter him in the cutting or the reined cow horse class. Which is his strongest event?" Pat watched him and I believe her level of amazement equaled mine.

"Why don't you enter him in both?" she asked.

"You can't do that! It's probably against the rules, but you just couldn't do it anyway."

I believed, as did most other Western trainers, that it was virtually impossible to ask a horse to mix the disciplines of cutting and reined cow work. Cutting requires the horse to stay back away from his cattle, preventing them from returning to the herd, while the reined cow horse has to go forward and control the animal. The two jobs contradict one another to such an extent that I know of no one who's ever thought they could be executed within the same time frame. Someone once told me that asking a reined cow horse to compete in the cutting was a little like asking a fox-hound to gather sheep.

Pat reminded me that she was the one who did most of the rule reading, and she couldn't remember anything prohibiting a horse from competing in both events at Salinas. We headed straight for the house, grabbed the little rulebook and began poring over it. Nowhere did it say that competing in both wasn't allowed! Pat filled out the form, entering Johnny in the 1964 Salinas competition in both the cutting and the working cow horse events.

Four or five days later, Pat called me at the stable and said that Lester Sterling was on the phone. Lester Sterling was a name from my past. He had been the chairman of the Salinas event for many years, ever since my childhood on the Salinas competition grounds. I knew this phone call wasn't going to be a comfortable one.

After I said hello, he shouted down the phone, "Have you gone mad? Monty, I've known you since you were born. I know you're not stupid, and I don't want you to embarrass yourself or our show. No horse can perform in both the cutting and the reined cow horse competition in the same week. It's just not possible!" He went on to say he had read the rules, and although they didn't preclude the entry, he just didn't feel he could let it happen.

I reminded him that the public did not view the preliminary competitions, and if the horses weren't good enough to move forward, the paying audience wouldn't have the opportunity to watch their performance. That would keep any embarrassment down to competitors and committee people. I told him I had my hands on a horse that wasn't about to embarrass anybody, anyway, and that if there was any embarrassment, it should be at the way Johnny had been shown in the past.

Lester Sterling allowed the entry. Johnny performed in front of two entirely separate sets of judges and under totally different circumstances. Sitting on his back, I felt I was in the presence of greatness. I didn't show him; he showed me, and the rest of the world, as well, that this business of being a working cow horse and a cutting horse in the same week was no problem, at least not for him. Johnny won both competitions and did it in a way that left no question about who the winner was. A large margin of points separated first and second in both contests.

The rules were changed immediately afterward. No horse has ever been allowed to repeat that double competition. I suppose it was a little like retiring the number of a Hall of Fame athlete. It seems fitting that Johnny Tivio is not only the first horse ever to accomplish the incredible feat but likely the only one.

Johnny Tivio went on to win four world championships and, in 1976, became one of the first horses to be inducted into the National Reined Cow Horse Association Hall of Fame. His trophies hang on our walls but I sometimes think, fancifully, that if our positions were reversed, there should be somewhere for Johnny to hang me up. He could show all the horses of the world how he was able to train a young horseman to perform at true world-class level.

I competed on Johnny Tivio in virtually every event where the horse carries a Western saddle, and he was world-class in all of them. Dean Oliver, arguably the greatest calf roper who ever lived, roped on Johnny several times and was amazed at his level of skill, even though the event was far from his specialty. I could go on telling stories about him until this book and two more are full, but there are two particular stories that exemplify just how overwhelming his talent was.

His unusual ability to perform in such a wide variety of contests led me, in 1964, to shoot for those championships they call All-Around. At one Class A Quarter Horse show, I entered him in everything in sight, including the event known as Western riding, which is a form of Western dressage. At that time, Western riding was new to the world of Quarter Horse shows, and while the elements of the discipline were present in the routines that preceded it, neither Johnny nor I had any experience with it as such. I had never trained him in Western riding and I had never shown a horse in that particular event. It involved flying lead changes, controlled walk, trot and canter, stopping, turning and backing up in some very precise ways.

Johnny and I were in the main arena, competing in the cutting, when there was an announcement that I was due in an outside ring to perform in Western riding. If I was to compete at all, they would have to wait for me. Pat was keeping a running record of where I stood in the race for the All-Around, or High-Point, Championship. She came to the side of the ring to tell me that if I did well in the cutting and placed in the Western riding, I would win the All-Around Championship—but it might be close.

I can't remember exactly where we finished in the cutting, either second or third. Pat met me at the out gate with the headgear necessary for the Western riding competition. We quickly changed the bridle and I trotted off to ring number two, where forty or fifty contestants were sitting in various stages of agitation. They had finished competing nearly half an hour before and were waiting for me to go through the course.

Clyde Kennedy was the judge. He was world-class and, as a trainer, had been responsible for many champions in both the Western and the hunter/jumper divisions. He was a superstar horseman who had been a qualified judge with the American Horse Shows Association for probably twenty years.

I remember riding into the ring as if it were yesterday. What happened during the next four minutes or so will never fade from my memory, nor will it fade from the memories of the other impatient competitors. I was a passenger on the greatest performance horse in the world. Clyde Kennedy marked him with the highest score he had ever given; it also turned out to be the highest score Johnny Tivio ever received. (Johnny matched it on one other occasion.) I was blown away, and so were some of the professional Western riding specialists, who simply could not believe it had been Johnny's first trip through the course.

I went on to show Johnny in twelve more Western riding competitions over the next two years, and to this day, his record in the event remains unbeaten. Johnny Tivio added another Register of Merit to his long list of awards thanks to the Western riding that we would not even have entered if it hadn't been for our desire to win the High-Point Championship.

With the creation of Flag Is Up Farms on the horizon, 1966 would be the last full year of competition for Johnny. It was a long and hard year for him; cutting was becoming very popular and the competition was getting tougher all the time, and the shows more numerous. I had set a goal of winning the cutting championship for the seven western states. We reduced the number of non-cutting competitions that we entered and went all out to achieve what virtually no horse had ever done before, which was to add this cutting championship to the reined cow horse championships he already had to his credit.

Johnny Tivio was the 1966 Champion Cutting Horse for the Pacific

Coast Cutting Horse Association, which included the seven western states. With that championship in hand, I set a new goal for us, which was to go to the American Quarter Horse Association finals at the Cow Palace and to close Johnny's career by winning the High-Point Championship there. This meant that we had to refocus our attention on a wide array of disciplines.

George A. Smith was still a 50 percent partner in Johnny, and he and his wife, Kathy, had had a lot of fun being involved in his incredible career. They came to the Cow Palace full of hope and support but also mindful of the challenges Johnny and I faced. We started slowly and by the midpoint we had achieved first in only one competition—the calf roping. I think I was

Johnny Tivio was never beaten in Western riding—he was the greatest!

about fourth in the cutting and third in the working cow horse. Don Dodge was sailing on a horse called Right Now and had three victories in the bag.

We were down to two contests: the open Western riding and the all-age reining. Johnny Tivio was never beaten in Western riding, so I was able to get one more first place under my belt before going to the final class.

The way the points were figured, the more horses that were in the class, the more points you got. As I recall, there were sixty-three performers in the pure reining. Johnny was a reined cow horse, not a specialist in pure reining. Since the best reiners in the United States were there, it appeared our chances were extremely slim. When I did the arithmetic, I realized we could win the High-Point, but only if we won first in that final reining competition. The Smiths came by and said they'd better get on the road, they had meetings in Sacramento. Obviously they didn't think we had a chance of winning the High-Point Championship.

Since my time with Brownie, I had developed a routine that I reserved for those moments in my career I felt were super important. I would ride my horse well away from everybody else and go through some exercises designed, I suppose, more for me than for my horse. The routine had to be rare so that I was not constantly asking myself, or my horse, for supernatural performance. Johnny Tivio understood this routine better than any other horse I have known. He seemed to comprehend the importance of the moment. The exercises might have seemed a waste of time to most professional trainers, but I felt that these quiet moments often placed our brain waves in sync.

If ever there was a need for this theory to work, it was then. I rode Johnny to a part of the Cow Palace complex that I will never forget. We went through the routine together and I felt we were prepared. I remember riding back toward the main arena with a renewed feeling of confidence. I could feel a quickening in Johnny's steps and an elevated resolve emanating from him. As our time to perform drew closer, I could run a video in my head of what we needed to do to win. I could see Johnny accomplishing an incredible routine, and there was a smile on my face as I rode into the arena.

With the championship in mind, a second-place finish would be no better than sixty-third. We went all out and our performance was virtually flawless. My smile just got larger. Johnny Tivio won first place, a saddle and a silver and gold belt buckle, presented to me by a man named Wes Eade. As he handed us our trophies, he said he'd just witnessed the impossible.

You can imagine what my telephone call to George Smith was like that evening. George was close to eighty years of age and was extremely happy with the unbelievable result. He said that Pat and I should be the sole owners of Johnny Tivio in retirement and we could pay him back from stallion fees. This was done within a year and Johnny belonged to us completely.

So Johnny, a Quarter Horse, stood at stud on a major Thoroughbred operation. While Thoroughbred people would think him inferior to their wonderful racehorses, Johnny was of the opinion that Flag Is Up was his property and that he was in charge of the activities there. We were able to give him his own field during the day and a comfortable stable at night. He also had his harem and, at just ten years of age, he could look forward to many years of contentment.

I rode Johnny often for the next seven or eight years, working cattle and surveying the farm with regularity. The champion Thoroughbred jockeys Bill Shoemaker and Lafitte Pincay also rode Johnny during his retirement and never forgot the experience. Pat would often choose Johnny to ride while instructing our three children in the skills of horsemanship.

People sometimes ask me if I think horses enjoy being ridden. I usually answer that it depends on who the rider is and how the riding is done. I tell them about Johnny and about how certain I am that he enjoyed every minute of being ridden. You don't have to be a genius to see when a horse is having fun. He made many trips to other ranches with Pat and me to gather cattle or ride through the mountains.

Johnny helped me in a profound manner with every horse that followed him, and I could fill a hundred pages with the details of those lessons. The most important thing I learned from Johnny, however, was that when he had been abused and forced, he didn't reach his full potential. When there was request rather than demand, and love instead of neglect, he was able to perform like no other horse before him. Not only is Johnny Tivio burned into my memory, but he has made an indelible mark on hundreds of Western trainers and certainly on the entire industry.

Retired on Flag Is Up Farms in 1968

My last hours with Johnny were, as you may imagine, some of the most bittersweet of my life. We all have to die, horse and human alike, but the lifespan of horses dictates that most of us will outlive our equine partners.

I was at Hollywood Park racetrack early one morning in April 1981, watching the racehorses train, and left for home at about ten. I arrived back at Flag Is Up sometime around one, drove directly to the farm office and met Pat as I came through the door. Immediately, I realized that something was very wrong. Pat embraced me.

"Johnny Tivio," she said through tears, "is dead."

Johnny had been in his pasture watching a mare being led past his field on her way to the breeding barn. He had stepped up on his toes and lifted his tail and was trotting along the roadway parallel with the mare when, all of a sudden, the men saw him drop like a stone. Dr. Van Snow, our resident veterinarian at the time, confirmed that he'd suffered a massive heart attack. Through my sadness, I was relieved that he had not suffered. In fact, you could say that he'd died smiling, thinking about that mare.

Johnny had been left where he'd fallen. As Pat and I walked toward his body, I could see his lifeless eyes. After a few minutes, Pat gave me a hug and walked away, realizing that I needed to spend time alone with Johnny. All the strength I'd felt from the fact that he hadn't suffered deserted me. I stayed there with Johnny Tivio, replaying in my mind the good times we'd had together. I tried to overcome my sorrow with the knowledge that I'd been the luckiest person in the world to have had this old friend. We'd shared many years together, and in recent times, Johnny had enjoyed the good life with a warm box stall and his beloved grass paddock from which he could see everything going on at the farm, including the mares moving to and from the breeding barn. Every time they passed him, Johnny became the big stallion again, calling out and traveling the length of his field like a three-year-old.

I walked around his body in the field, reliving contests won and lost, talking to him about times funny and sad. I felt like a child, and it seemed that revisiting these memories would somehow keep his life from leaving. His life has never left me, and I, as well as those around me, will be forever affected by the time he was with us. I remember kneeling behind him and lying over his shoulders.

As he lay collapsed on his side, with that heavy, final weight that only death brings, I knew where to bury him. For some time, I'd had it in mind to make a special graveyard just in front of the farm office, where I would give each horse his own headstone with an engraved bronze plaque with the horse's name, dates and a line or two about his qualities or personality. Johnny Tivio would be the first to be buried there.

I dug his grave myself, using the farm's backhoe. By the time I was finished, it was dark, but the hole was dug and Johnny Tivio's body had to be lowered into it. This was the toughest part. I knew I would never again have a friend like Johnny, and I could not bring myself to cover him with earth; I couldn't do it. Dr. Snow volunteered to carry on while I went up to the house and crawled underneath the covers.

A few days later, when Pat was sending Johnny's American Quarter Horse registration papers to the association to inform them of his death, she made an amazing discovery. Johnny had died on his twenty-fifth birthday. The plaque on his gravestone reads: "Johnny Tivio, April 24, 1956 to April 24, 1981. Known to all as the greatest all-around working horse ever to enter an arena."

Johnny Tivio had seemed to want to please me in whatever way he could. I think he believed he was the only horse in my life. He never knew there would be a Lomitas, a Shy Boy or a Dually. No horse can speak the language of humans, but I believe that if Johnny could have talked to me at the time of his death, he would have told me to get busy. I think he would have said that his life was over; he was out of here, but I should go forward with the lessons he'd taught me. Johnny would have reminded me how dedicated he'd been to being the best he could be, and he'd have admonished me to take on that same state of mind for myself. He might have told me to stop mourning him and start making things better for horses and for people using the techniques he'd worked so hard to teach me. The fact is that thousands of horses and people have benefited from the lessons he provided.

I hope that Johnny Tivio knows about this book, wherever he is now. I hope he knows I met the Queen of England and that I've toured the world demonstrating the techniques I've discovered during a long life of horsemanship. I hope he knows he's the last horse in this book because the best is always saved for last. Johnny Tivio, you were the best—you were *great!*

CONCLUSION

When I look back, I can see how horse after horse carried me away from cruelty and toward kindness and understanding. The lessons I learned from the horses in my life form the basis of all my work and of the message I want to pass on to the world.

I was still a young boy when I first encountered the no-name mustang, who taught me the language of equus. Without words, he told me it was unnecessary to treat horses harshly or cruelly, or to use the methods of my father and his forefathers, which are still too often employed today. It isn't necessary to break a horse's spirit, to dominate or subdue him. On the contrary, such techniques can be proved to be absolutely counterproductive. That realization led me to a lifetime's effort to improve the relationship between man and horse.

I've spent decades working toward banning whips in racing. While there has been a dramatic reduction in their use, there is strong resistance to banning them completely. Hey Sam, Prince of Darkness, Stanley and many others have encouraged me, through their memory, to continue with this effort. The Dually halter and the Monty Roberts starting-gate blanket are products of lessons taught me by these tolerant individuals. I owe the wonderful horses of the world my undying efforts to create a better environment for them.

Since 1996, when my first book was launched, I have been fortunate to receive many awards, including, on January 29, 1998, the Founder's Award from the American Society for the Prevention of Cruelty to Animals. The awards have various titles but each of them is connected in some way to the horses in my life. I am the recipient of these gifts but the credit belongs to the horses.

My books and videos have provided me with the opportunity to deal with misunderstood and mistreated horses on a global basis. While most people want to be fair with our equine partners, the actions of the uninformed can often create a horse's psychological problems. It appears that I have accepted the role of spokesman for the horse, to bring to the world methods that replace violence with communication and understanding.

As I write this, I am preparing for a trip to Sydney, Australia, where the use of whips behind the starting gate has recently been banned. I am excited about presenting options to the racing fraternity of that country. Perhaps Australia can be a model to encourage many countries to take up the same cause.

It is my dream to live long enough to see the majority of horsemen working in partnerships rather than slave/master relationships. I long for the day when the horse-and-human connection can be experienced so as to leave the horse with his dignity. Each individual I have included in this book has led me to yearn for a time when horsemen find joy in watching the generosity of horses with the freedom of choice. Relationships such as I have had with horses will lead to green pastures in retirement instead of cold-hearted destruction at the end of their careers.

Perhaps most important, I developed from my understanding of the language of equus the technique I called join-up. Mustangs in the wild taught me how to emulate their gestures so I could let them know they could trust me. The results were startling, but even I underestimated the power of join-up. The mustang mare not only trusted me but also protected me from perceived danger as if I were her infant. The irony is that while I can communicate with horses, humans tend to disbelieve what they see. You might think it would be easier to communicate with people but, in fact, egos and traditions often get in the way.

The horses told me I was right—boy, did they tell me! The lessons those mustangs taught me early in life carried me forward into a successful career, not only in rodeo and Western disciplines but also in the Thoroughbred racing industry, to a level I would never have believed possible. An Act, Alleged and Lomitas—these are just a few of the horses that are burned into my memory. The mustangs, however, were closer to nature than the elite individuals, and it was because of their lessons that I was allowed to succeed in world-class competition.

Julia's Doll taught me the need to keep an open mind and let the horse show you where her talent lies. The lessons of Rough Frolic were to show me that the most effective trainer is the one who stays out of the way of a good horse. Observe him in action, respect his choices and he will eventually be a champion. My Blue Heaven and Johnny Tivio were crystal clear in their efforts to show me that the great trainer does not *make* the horse perform—he causes the horse to *want to*.

Her Majesty the Queen of England changed everything. She validated join-up and sent me on a tour of the United Kingdom and Ireland—and suddenly people started to believe what was happening before their eyes. Since the day I saw the Queen Mother with tears streaming down her face at the sight of her filly being started with my methods, I've been on a non-stop mission to demonstrate join-up to as many people as possible around the world. I am training instructors in every quarter of the globe to take my message forward. Soon, another generation will be doing the work better than I ever could.

This book has been a pleasure to write. I have relived dramas and crises, intense emotions, valleys and certainly peaks. I feel a deep humility about the experiences the horses in my life have given me, and it is my fervent hope that I can pass on these experiences to generations to come.

GLOSSARY

Acute laminitis A condition of inflammation of the soft tissues within the hard wall of a horse's hoof.

Breaking in The act of causing a horse to accept its first saddle, bridle and rider while using what are considered to be traditional methods.

Bulldogging Also known as steer wrestling. A rodeo competition in which the primary cowboy stops a steer by leaping from his horse and wrestling it to the ground.

Cutting The sorting of cattle. It generally refers to separating one animal at a time from the herd while on horseback.

Disunited The horse's legs are used in the wrong sequence while cantering—the leading leg in front is opposite to the leading leg behind.

Dually™ halter The trademarked name of a particular halter invented by the author. With the use of the Dually™, numerous problems with horses can be addressed and fixed without pain or violence. The halter allows the handler to school an initially uncooperative horse. When the horse resists the Dually, it becomes smaller and less comfortable, and when he cooperates, the Dually gives immediate reward by expanding and becoming quite comfortable. Through its use, the handler can communicate with the horse, and willingness and relaxation will be achieved. Recently, an invention called a Gentle Leader has emerged on the scene to assist in the training and handling of man's best friend, the dog. A Gentle Leader acts upon a set of principles similar to the Dually.

Flight animal An animal whose primary defense is to flee. Flight animals are usually herbivores and seldom resort to violence if flight is an alternative.

Flying changes, lead changes A change of leading leg while remaining at the canter, performed while all four legs are off the ground. The front and hind legs must change at the same time. Horses that cannot achieve a smooth flying change tend to be disunited and are less athletic in their work. It is a requirement of coordinated movement to travel on the right lead while making a turn to the right, and the left lead for a turn to the left.

Gaited horses A group of animals that have been trained or find it natural to have gaits (methods of locomotion) other than the natural walk, trot and canter.

Ground manners A term used to describe the behavioral patterns of horses toward people interacting with them on the ground or otherwise off their back.

Group I race A race qualified by international racing secretaries as being superior to a Group II race. This is the highest level of racing for Thoroughbreds.

Group II race A race qualified by international racing secretaries as being superior to a Group III race.

Group III race A race qualified by international racing secretaries as being superior to a stakes race and carrying the classification, Gr. III.

Group winner A winner of any race with a Group status in its title.

Hackamore A bitless bridle, requiring a high degree of responsiveness from the horse.

Handicap race A contest where the participants are allocated a certain level of weight they must carry. The racing secretary at the track in question determines these weights.

Haze horse The mount of the hazer—the secondary cowboy—in bulldogging. The role of the haze horse is to keep the steer moving in a straight line.

In hand Leading rather than riding a horse. Competitions that are based on conformation, style and turnout are conducted in hand. The horse is shown with just a halter and no other tack.

International rating A numerical score allocated to a Thoroughbred racehorse. This is usually arrived at with a voting system of the international racing secretaries.

Lead or leading leg The front leg with which the horse leads while cantering. The horse may have to change the leading leg (flying change) when moving round to the left or right. Horses moving in a left arc will travel more comfortably with the left legs reaching double the distance of the right legs. The opposite is true if the horse is negotiating a right arc.

Lunging ring An enclosure (usually round) used for training or exercising horses.

Maiden race A race for horses that have not won a previous race.

Piaffelike movement Best described as prancing in place—actually, a trot without forward movement.

Quarter Horse One of a breed of strong saddle horses developed in the western United States and originally trained for quarter-mile races.

Scratches A term used to describe a fungus condition usually affecting the area just above and to the rear of the hoof. Scratches could be compared to athlete's foot as a human equivalent.

Stakes race A race advertised prior to any given race meet, offering money added without the effect of wagering, and internationally accepted as a high quality contest.

Superior mudder A horse that performs best when the surface is muddy or deep.

Turnout An enclosure used to release a horse in. Turnouts may have grass or sand and are usually less than an acre but larger than one-eighth of an acre.

Western riding competition A group of contests for horses ridden in a Western saddle, such as cutting, reining, working cow horse, pleasure and trail.

ACKNOWLEDGMENTS

This is the fifth book that my wife, Pat, and I have worked on together. Amazingly, we discovered that Pat knew every one of the horses in my life with one exception, my first horse, Ginger. I thank Pat from the bottom of my heart for throwing her enthusiasm and endless hours into helping me put the stories together. She was my sounding board, my typist and my editor. She gathered photos from all over the world and from our archives so readers could have visuals of those special horses. Without Pat, it would have been impossible for me to complete *The Horses in My Life* given the many days I am away from home. When necessary, she even traveled with me, computer in hand, and together we made it happen.

Three people were willing to read the manuscript while it was still a "work in progress." Michael Schwartz, Sally King and Lee Rosenberg deserve special thanks, as they were the ones who volunteered for the first read and were responsible for exceptionally good input. To my English tour team, the instructors and students from the Monty Roberts International Learning Center, I send my thanks for your helpful suggestions.

Jane Turnbull, my English literary agent, has worked tirelessly to make sure we found the right publishers to obtain the largest readership from my first book onward. Thanks, Jane, for being a staunch believer and for your pursuit of the perfect publishing company who not only believe in my concepts but also believe in me.

Louise Dennys, executive vice president of Random House of Canada, has been with me from my very first book and is now publishing the fifth book in Canada. I thank her for her steadfast kindness and support. Thank you, Anne Collins, publisher of Random House Canada, for your belief in this project. Also, Pat and I wish to thank Stacey Cameron for her generous time and effort to make this book the very best it can be. She has been a tough but effective taskmaster, but we appreciate her hard work and dedication, and feel she succeeded with all our goals. It is a pleasure to work with someone who cares enough to maximize efforts to reach excellence.

Caroline Robbins, publisher of Trafalgar Square Publishing, is a long-time friend, and it is with great pleasure that we finally have the opportunity to work together on a book in the United States. Caroline and Martha Cook, managing editor, have been invaluable over the years in assisting with many of my literary efforts. Caroline has been a friend of the horse industry for decades. She has orchestrated a marriage of book publishing and the world of horses more effectively than anyone else I have known. Thank you, Caroline and Martha.

I want to acknowledge the rest of my family, who help keep "the balls in the air": daughter Debbie and son-in-law Tom Loucks. I know I don't say thank you enough for what you do, so I'm publicly saying thank you now. You help Pat and me make it happen. Thank you, daughter Laurel, for always caring and for your unconditional love.

PHOTO CREDITS
We would like to thank the following
for kindly supplying photographs for use in the book:

T. Abahzy: 99, 105, 131, 136; Si Almond: 12; R.A. Anderson: 58;
George Axt: iii, 63, 229; Bancroft Photography: 199; APRH P. Bertrand et
fils: 146; Click: 40–1; Christopher Dydyk: 223; June Fallow: 50, 53, 66,
76, 84, 232, 236, 239; Gestüt Fährhof: 191, 193 (top and bottom right),
194; Helene Glassman: vi, vii; Jan Heine: 173; Milne: 34–5, 70-71; Frank
Nolting: viii, 186, 193 (bottom left), 196; Jim Raftery: 103, 119; Pat
Roberts: 144, 164, 165; Gisela Schregle: 217; Lavoy Sheppard: 212;
J. Sorby: 113; Frank Sorge Fotograph: 195; Claus-Jörg Tuchel: 188;
Dr. Van Snow: 152; Lee Walsh: 20; John Wiester: 124–25

FOR FURTHER INFORMATION

My goal is to leave the world a better place for horses and people than
I found it. In that effort I invite you to contact us at

Tel: 805 688 4382
E-mail: admin@montyroberts.com
www.montyroberts.com

for further information regarding clinics, conferences, educational
videos and other educational material, including my four
previously published books:

The Man Who Listens to Horses
Shy Boy: The Horse that Came in from the Wild
Horse Sense for People
From My Hands to Yours